Basics of Singing

Second Edition

Basics of Singing

Jan Schmidt

SCHIRMER BOOKS
A DIVISION OF MACMILLAN, INC.
New York

Schirmer Books
A Division of Macmillan, Inc.
866 Third Avenue, New York, N.Y. 10022

Collier Macmillan Canada, Inc.

Library of Congress Catalog Card Number:

Printed in the United States of America

printing number
1 2 3 4 5 6 7 8 9 10

Library of Congress Cataloging in Publication Data

Basics of singing.

   Principally songs with piano acc. and chord symbols;
some of the songs are in both high- and low-voice
versions.
   English, German, or Italian words.
   Bibliography: p.
   Includes index.
   Contents: Technique—Song anthology.
   1. Singing—Methods.   2. Songs with piano.
I. Schmidt, Jan, 1942–
MT825.B27   1989   88-753172
ISBN 0-02-872341-4

to those members of my family who have supported and encouraged my study of music

Contents

Song Anthology Contents

FOLK SONGS

SONGS FROM MUSICAL THEATER

ART SONGS AND ARIAS

ROUNDS

Preface

This book is intended as a text and anthology for beginning and intermediate singing students enrolled in a class or individual voice study at the college or university level. To be most helpful, it should be used under the supervision of a competent teacher, who will adapt and amplify its contents.

Information in the body of the text is meant to be direct and easily understood. As can be seen in the bibliography, it is compiled from some of the most authoritative sources available. The illustrations, although simplified for clarity of understanding, are anatomically correct.

The forty-five songs in the anthology, featuring many new selections for the current edition, are divided into three categories: fifteen from the folk idiom, fifteen from musical theater, and fifteen art songs and arias. The songs are highly appealing to the contemporary student and valuable as tools for voice building. All songs are printed in keys of comfortable singing ranges. Some songs appear in high and low keys, so that a single edition of this text will serve all voices.

Also available with the second edition are practice tapes containing accompaniments for all songs present in the anthology. Although, for the sake of his own self-sufficiency, a student should strive to play song melodies himself, it is hoped that the tapes will assist those who have not yet mastered adequate keyboard skills. For songs which require them, brief and unpublished piano introductions have been supplied. Foreign language texts have been recorded before the "High Voice" accompaniment of songs to which they relate.

Finally, please note the rounds at the conclusion of the anthology, useful in developing singers' harmonic independence. The singing of rounds is often a helpful and entertaining step to building confidence in ensemble singing.

Acknowledgments

Special words of appreciation are offered here for the special instruction in voice performance and vocal pedagogy offered by my two principal teachers, William Vennard and Robert Bernard. Thanks also to James Low and Dennis Castellano for their assistance in the selection of art songs and theater songs respectively, to Maebeth Guyton, Mary Maude Moore, Jean Shackleton, and Ramona Mathewson for their contributions to the anthology, and to Sara McFerrin for her evaluation of the text. I am deeply grateful to all voice teachers and coaches who submitted ideas for the second edition of this text and hope they will find resulting changes responsive to their classroom and studio requirements.

Part One: TECHNIQUE

1 Practicing

Learning to sing is a slow and patient undertaking, in which a good ear is the prerequisite, the imagery is an aid supplied by the teacher, and the experience is gradually accumulated until it is so powerful that merely calling up the memory will reproduce it.

In his book, *Singing, The Mechanism and the Technic,* William Vennard wrote the foregoing quote, which seems to be as appropriate a statement to consider as any when one begins a formalized study of singing. Perhaps the words "slow," "patient," and "gradually" should be capitalized. At least, they should be stressed in the student's mind, as should be the necessity of faith in the teacher. The teacher will tailor the suggestions made in this or any other text to a student's particular needs, thus rendering it considerably more valuable.

Singing is a learned skill, and all those with sufficient motivation and intelligence can improve their performance considerably if they commit themselves to it. When it is finally learned, singing is a thoroughly comfortable and enjoyable experience. It's more than that—it's exciting! But as one first makes an effort at voice training, it is often confusing and sometimes excruciatingly embarrassing, emotions that eventually pass, after enough performances have been sung. Students are asked to make sounds they cannot easily make, and when they are finally assured by the teacher that they are indeed succeeding, they often dislike what they hear, or simply feel that a tone is strange. That is where the patience is required.

The slowness of learning to sing correctly refers to the great amount of experimentation the student needs to do, both under the teacher's supervision and, particularly, in private practice. Improving one's singing is a never-ending project for most professionals and many amateurs. Mastering the basic skills for a "solid" singing technique for popular, theater, or classical music takes years, not months. It is similar to learning a new sport, in the sense that the

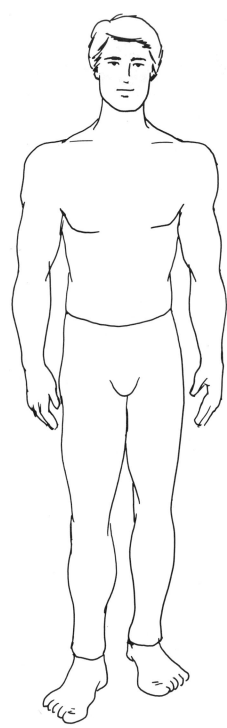

FIGURE 1.1
Correct stance for singing

coordination of numerous muscles is involved. Therefore, for some time, students should expect more "misses" than "hits." When one also realizes that techniques for styling and presentation must be learned as well, an understanding of the size of the task begins to develop.

As students continue to work at building their singing voice, they gain a progressively clearer concept of what to expect from themselves. That this concept is aided enormously by the ear is obvious, but students also begin to recognize and memorize the physical sensations they experience when singing correctly. "Singing by feeling" is especially noticeable as they sing in more and more varied circumstances and the acoustics change with each room and situation.

In order to make adequate progress, the singer must practice carefully and consistently. Since, in such areas as lower jaw and throat positions, the student is often dealing with adjustments involving a fraction of an inch, it can readily be seen that concentration must be exclusively on singing. As many distractions as possible must be eliminated. If, at first, concentration does not extend beyond ten minutes, stop practicing! For without concentration, the beginning voice student will slip back into the familiar—and probably incorrect—manner of singing. It is better to do several short, concentrated practice sessions in a day than to do more lengthy, unfocused sessions.

There are numerous approaches to teaching singing, and many can be successful, but most teachers would agree that practicing should be done in a solitary, quiet place, and always in a standing position. This means that practicing while driving from place to place is not particularly helpful to voice building; neither is trying to sing quietly in an apartment or dormitory room. If practice facilities are not available, public buildings with pianos, such as churches, often are. And their proprietors are usually cooperative in letting students use rooms and instruments.

The generally accepted stance for a good singing posture is as follows (see also Figure 1.1).

The feet should be planted firmly on the floor, slightly apart (approximately twelve inches [300 mm.]), one slightly ahead of the other. The weight should be on the forward portion of the feet, to allow greater flexibility in breathing, and also to create a more energetic impression when one sings for an audience.

The knees should be slightly bent, to allow the singer to stand as firmly as possible. It often happens that one is inadvertently pushed or bumped during a rehearsal or performance, and, to say nothing of the benefits good posture provides for good voice production, a secure stance is definitely to a singer's advantage.

The shoulders should be firmly back and down, neither tense nor drooping. A differentiation should be made here between this position and the extremely low shoulder position required of dancers.

The arms should hang at the sides in a very relaxed manner, slightly bent at the elbows. This bend creates a less militaristic look than would perfectly straight arms.

The hands of new singing students often tend to express the nervousness they are feeling. Many people, therefore, find it helpful, particularly during lessons, to place the fingertips firmly on the sides of the thighs and to keep them there.

The neck should be relaxed both in front and in back and should not be turned even the slightest degree. Because of unconscious head movement, the neck is frequently stretched in various directions, so special attention should be given to guarding against this. It will prevent straining of the muscles from which the voice box is suspended.

The head position should be determined by the focus of the eyes, which should be straight ahead. Being aware that the neck is relaxed will also help to ensure that the head is neither too far back nor too far forward. Generally, the chin should be parallel to the floor.

Essentially, there are four pieces of equipment that are of incalculable assistance to the singer. They are two mirrors, a penlight, and a cassette tape recorder. The mirrors should be of two kinds: one, full length, from which the student can gauge overall posture and appearance, with the second a small hand mirror, with which throat position can be evaluated. The penlight can be shined into the mouth and throat to greatly facilitate the observation with the hand mirror. The tape recorder should be used to make an auditory check on performance progress.

To listen to oneself can be terribly uncomfortable, but there is perhaps no quicker method of correcting a mistake than to hear it when it is played back, and to recognize it as coming from an external source. The recording limitations of the machine cause the voice to sound considerably less sonorous than it actually is, but it is nevertheless a valuable aid to practicing. If students do not have a piano available for use, or do not know how to play one, they can, and should, record vocal exercises and songs given to them by their teacher.

Again, practicing, to progress as quickly as possible, demands absolute concentration and attention to the smallest details. If there is a more efficient or beautiful way to sing a note, stop and try it again. Those with the most to gain from paying attention to details are the singers themselves. If concentration falters, relax for a few minutes, then resume your practicing. A beginning voice student is generally able to practice for thirty minutes, maintaining concentration and exercising the voice, without tiring.

2 Vocalizing

Every practice session should begin with a period of vocalizing, exercising, or "warming up" the voice. If a student is planning to practice for thirty minutes, for example, half of that time might well be allocated to *vocalises* (vocal exercises) and half to the study of songs. The reason for vocalizing can be more readily understood when the student realizes that the vocal cords are actually muscles that extend from the front to the back of the throat, and that, in fact, one is learning to coordinate the action of these, as well as of other muscles in the *larynx* (voice box), with one's airstream. Vocalises will increase blood circulation, flexibility, and responsiveness, characteristics that can then be transferred to the songs.

Voice students need to understand how the body participates in the singing process. Because such an understanding aids in analyzing reasons for desirable and undesirable voice production, some simplified drawings (Figures 2.1–2.4), augmented by discussion, are included here.

Vertically, the adult larynx measures about one and a half inches (40 mm.). The average measurement of its circumference is five inches (125 mm.). At puberty, the male larynx sometimes enlarges more dramatically than does the female, accounting for the difficulty in coordinating the actions of the laryngeal muscles often experienced by teenage boys.

The larynx is composed of two major cartilages—*cartilage* being that bodily substance that can develop into bone—namely, the cricoid and the thyroid. The *cricoid* is actually a specialized cartilaginous ring at the upper end of the windpipe. It is shaped like a signet ring, with the signet in the back of the throat and the shaft of the ring in the front of the throat. The *thyroid,* which we frequently identify as the Adam's apple, is V-shaped, with the angle of the V in the front of the throat, and the open portion in the back.

The *vocal cords,* also called *vocal folds,* attach to the thyroid cartilage in the front, stretch backward across the path of the airstream, and attach to the two small *ary-*

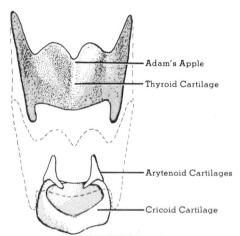

FIGURE 2.1
Front view of the separated cartilages of the larynx

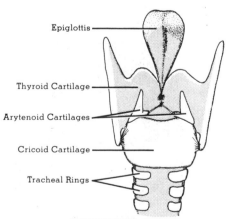

FIGURE 2.2
Back view of the larynx

7

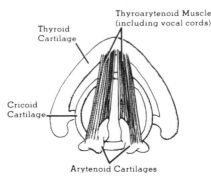
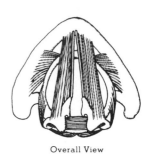

FIGURE 2.3
Muscles inside the larynx

tenoids, pyramid-shaped cartilages, in the back. These small cartilages sit upon the upper edge of the cricoid, gliding along its surface. Because of the action of the laryngeal muscles, these cartilages approach each other and the vocal cords are brought together.

There are, in all, five groups of muscles in the larynx, including the vocal cords, or *thyroarytenoids,* named for the cartilages to which they attach, and ten cartilages. Only the leaf-shaped epiglottis, readily seen in the drawings, might well be mentioned at this stage of study. It is of particular interest because of its size and shape and because of its function. It lies back across the top of the larynx frequently during swallowing, diverting food particles across the windpipe, into the esophagus.

Now to the practical points of vocalization.

In the following paragraphs, a set of progressive vocalises will be given. The possibility exists for devising literally hundreds of vocalises, most of which might be used advantageously. It is important to realize precisely for what reason a vocalise is used. For the beginning student, a fairly set and limited number of exercises might be the preferable regimen. Again, they should be worked on for at least fifteen minutes before proceeding to the practice of songs.

A well-produced sung tone is based on what is often termed an "open" throat. The process for learning this technique can be accelerated by using the *oh* vowel for a period of time instead of the *ah* vowel. The *oh* vowel more quickly enables the singer to get used to an elevated soft palate (the muscular portion of the roof of the mouth, directly behind the hard palate) and the lowered tongue, the two primary indicators of an open throat. It is also true that most new voice students do not stretch open the throat to the extent that they imagine, and the *oh* will counteract this tendency.

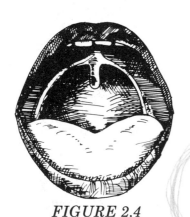

FIGURE 2.4
Open throat position

Vocalises

EXERCISE 2.1.

Silently yawn the throat open, and at the beginning stage of the yawn, quietly slide from your highest comfortable pitch to your lowest comfortable pitch on the vowel *oh* or *ah*. Using a hand mirror and penlight in this and all succeeding exercises, be certain the tongue and palate remain absolutely still. Repeat.

ah

Proceeding in a similar manner, begin a yawn, slide from your lowest comfortable pitch to your highest comfortable pitch, then back down to your lowest comfortable pitch.

ah

Goal: To maintain a constantly high palate and lowered tongue and an even, unbroken tone.

Avoid: The arching tongue, lowering palate, breaks in the tone. Be careful not to use the full part of the yawn, or the throat will be too widely opened, resulting in a depressed tongue and "gagging" sensation.

EXERCISE 2.2.

Using the same method required in the first vocalise, and proceeding in this and all vocalises upward by half steps, slide between pitches of a perfect fifth on the *oh* or *ah* vowel. All exercises should be developed to as high a pitch as is comfortable; then descend by half steps back to the original starting pitch. This arrangement is used because the vocal cords are more relaxed on low pitches than they are on high ones.

ah

Goal: Same as Exercise 2.1.

Avoid: Same as Exercise 2.1.

EXERCISE 2.3.

Retaining the "open" throat on the *oh* or *ah* vowel, and sliding between pitches, sing the following pitches.

ah _____

Goal: Same as exercises 2.1 and 2.2. Also listen for a consistent, unchanging vowel throughout the range of the vocalise.

Avoid: The same undesirable characteristics mentioned for exercises 2.1 and 2.2. Be careful to eliminate *h*'s between notes, by paying more attention to sliding.

EXERCISE 2.4.

Using the same directions given for Exercise 2.3, slide through octaves. Introducing a very slight nasal quality by thinking the syllable *on,* as in "honk," into the vowel in the extreme high and low pitches will facilitate the singing of this vocalise.

ah _____

Goal: To maintain a constant vowel, uninterrupted tone and consistent volume level throughout the range of the exercise. This exercise is also helpful in developing a wider singing range.

Avoid: The changing vowel, *h*'s, and lowering volume between pitches.

EXERCISE 2.5.

To further develop range, use the *oh* or *ah* vowel to slide through arpeggios.

ah _____

Goal: Same as Exercise 2.4.

Avoid: Same as Exercise 2.4.

EXERCISE 2.6.

To assist in accelerating the airflow, sing the following exercise, teeth apart, lower lip lightly touching upper teeth for the initial *vee* sound. Conceive of the pitches as raising instead of lowering, so that the airflow will continue to move energetically.

vee _____

Goal: To transcend the "breathy" phase of voice production until a brilliant "core" is consistently sung into the tone. It will often cause a feeling of vibration in the head, called "head tone" and "ringing in the ears."

Avoid: Singing with clenched teeth and a fluctuating amount of brilliance.

EXERCISE 2.7.

To clarify more fully the tongue positions required for the different vowels, sing the following vowel series on a single pitch. The vowels should be sung with low jaw and high palate and should seem to "melt" into one another. The tip of the tongue should be in approximately the same place for the *ee* and *ay* vowels. For most students, "head tone" should be felt in the same place as the vowels progress.

Ee   Ay   Ah   Oh   Oo

Goal: Same as Exercise 2.6.

Avoid: Same as Exercise 2.6.

3 Breathing

As soon as the principle of the open throat has been clearly understood and somewhat integrated into the vocalises, the basics of good breath support, perhaps the most important single element in the production of beautiful tone, should be reviewed. The open throat was discussed first, because, when blown against a tight throat, an energetic airstream, regardless of its amount of control, can create discomfort and hoarseness.

Beginning with the physiological process of breathing (see Figure 3.1), the windpipe, or *trachea,* is made up of a series of cartilaginous rings somewhat resembling a vacuum hose. It is about four and a half inches (114 mm.) long, with an average diameter of three-quarters of an inch (19 mm.). Connecting the rings are muscle and membrane. The same membranous tissue also covers the larynx, throat, mouth, and nose—important information when considering the effects of upper-respiratory infections. The trachea eventually subdivides into two *bronchi,* one bronchus for each lung. The bronchi further subdivide into numerous *bronchioles,* through which oxygen passes into the lungs.

The *lungs* are made of spongy membranous tissue, which is formed into two sacs, one located in the right side of the chest, the other in the left. Oxygen passes through these membranes into the blood. The lungs also dispose of certain waste products, such as carbon dioxide. They can expand their capacity only as far as the ribs will allow, which is one reason why it is important for singers to keep the position of the ribs raised and out. In a cycle of deep inhalation and exhalation, such as is used in singing, three and a half quarts (3.3 liters) of air may be exhaled, leaving one and a half quarts (1.4 liters) of residual air in the lungs. Because new singing students often operate on the premise of "saving air" while they sing, which is nearly always a mistake,

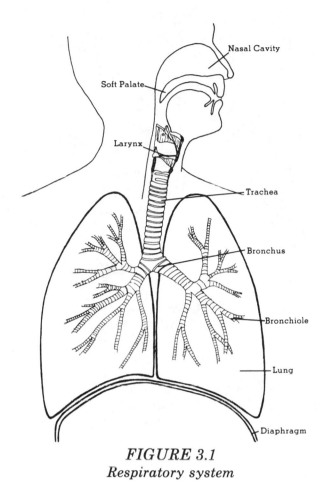

FIGURE 3.1
Respiratory system

it is important to be aware of the large quantity of air that can and should be used.

Assisting in the raising and lowering of the ribs are the *intercostal* muscles (see Figure 3.2). The backward and downward position of the shoulders also enables the ribs to be positioned most optimally for maximum lung expansion. The ribs should be maintained in this expanded condition during exhalation as well as inhalation, in order to prevent their weight from prematurely pushing air out of the lungs.

Below the lungs lies the *diaphragm*. It is a massive, dome-shaped muscle, which divides the chest cavity from the abdominal cavity (see Figure 3.1). It attaches to the lower ribs and vertebrae, with its dome pointing up toward the chest cavity. It is the most important muscle of inhalation. As one inhales, the diaphragm flattens, allowing the lungs to inflate. One consequence of this action is that—and singers should take careful note of it—during inhalation, the abdominal muscles will move outward as the abdominal contents are compressed by the lowering of the diaphragm.

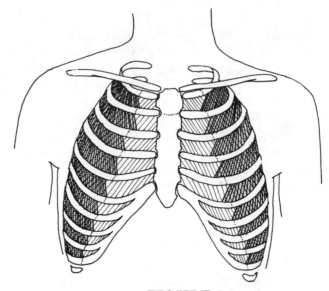

FIGURE 3.2
Internal and external
intercostal muscles

Conversely, at exhalation, which occurs while a tone is being produced, the general direction of the abdominal muscles
will usually be movement inward (see Figure 3.3). Most new

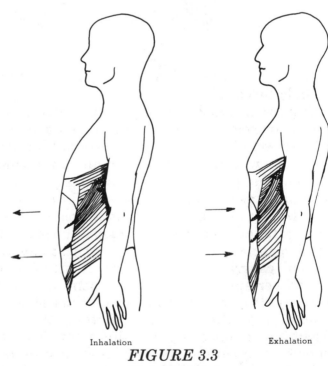

Inhalation   Exhalation

FIGURE 3.3
Muscle action
during breathing

voice students move their abdominal muscles in exactly the opposite direction from that which is ideal.

As the muscles of the chest are most active at inhalation, so the muscles of the abdomen are most active at exhalation. There are four groups of abdominal muscles, all of which are called into action during singing. As can be seen in Figure 3.4, the area covered by the abdominals extends from the breastbone *(sternum)* and ribs to the pubic bone and around to the back. It is important that they be relaxed during inhalation throughout their total expanse, to allow maximum intake of air.

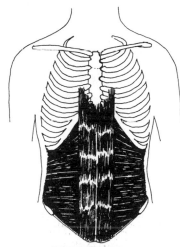

FIGURE 3.4
Muscles of the abdomen

For an even release of air, the singer may influence diaphragmatic movement by flexible and smooth contraction of the abdominals during exhalation. Although it is typical of "well-supported" singing to feel muscular exertion in the back, a new student might pull in the abdominal muscles too rapidly, resulting in discomfort. To avoid this occurrence and to keep the pressure of the rising abdominal contents off the diaphragm for as long as possible, the singer should be certain that inward abdominal movement is paced with the musical phrase. It should be slow and gradual unless an increased amount of air is needed to produce a higher or louder pitch. When this situation occurs, the rising diaphragm will push air out of the lungs with more force if the abdominals are pulled in more quickly.

Now that the mechanics of breathing have been discussed, the voice-building process will be helped by reviewing the vocalises listed in Chapter 2 with an expanded view of their purpose. In addition to the concentration on the open throat, careful breathing habits should be observed. That is, the abdominals should be expanded at inhalation and move gradually inward as the vocalises progress. Once exhalation is begun, the inward movement should be continuous, including the "spaces" between the notes. Stopping the pulling action after each pitch results in a "punchy-sounding" vocal line, instead of a smooth one.

The ribs should be kept in an upward and outward position during inhalation and exhalation. The shoulders should be kept back and down, never moving, during inhalation and exhalation. Finally, a check can be made on this process, by placing the palms of the hands on the abdomen, fingers spread, to monitor the movement of the abdominals throughout their length. When breathing is efficient, the result will be a flexible, uninterrupted tone. After having reviewed the vocalises in Chapter 2 (Exercises 2.1–2.7) with a new emphasis on breathing, concentrate on the following (Exercises 3.1–3.5).

Vocalises

EXERCISE 3.1.

At the rate of one exhalation per second, and using the *hoh* or *hah* syllable, speak the sounds while rapidly pulling in the abdominal muscles. It is important to allow the abdominals to relax (move outward) after each syllable.

Hah   Hah   Hah   Hah
(in) (out) (in) (out) (in) (out) (in) (out)

Goal: To develop a strong, even contraction of the abdominal muscles over their entire area.

Avoid: Singing with a high jaw and neglecting to let the abdominals relax between syllables (the consequence of which is muscular spasm).

EXERCISE 3.2.

Using the "open throat" and keeping the lower jaw down and back, sing the arpeggio given, on *staccato,* or short, notes.

Hah   Hah   Hah   Hah   Hah

Goal: To add facility to the pattern of abdominal movement established in the vocalise in Exercise 3.1.

Avoid: Same difficulties discussed in Exercise 3.1.

EXERCISE 3.3.

For greater flexibility, sing the following pattern using the *oh* or *ah* vowel with an unbroken *(legato)* line of absolutely consistent quality. Use the concept of sliding from pitch to pitch. Add very slight nasality on the upper and lower tones for greater ease of performance and to give more fullness to sound. The first pitch in each group of three should be slightly accented, by rapidly contracting, then relaxing, the abdominal muscles.

Goal: To coordinate the activity of the abdominal muscles with the airflow, resulting in a flexible, smooth line.

Avoid: Fluctuating volume level and interrupted flow of tone.

EXERCISE 3.4.

To develop volume, sustain a single pitch for sixteen beats, at a moderate tempo, using the *oh* or *ah* vowel. Gradually increase the volume to the loudest comfortable level, then gradually decrease to the original level, always pulling inward on the abdominals. Blow out air more rapidly as volume builds.

Goal: To fluctuate volume levels, using an unbroken line and an evenly distributed progression of sound.

Avoid: Sacrificing tone as the volume level is altered because of a changing vowel or an erratic vibrato.

EXERCISE 3.5.

Repeat Exercise 2.1, in both its parts, to relax cords.

4 Learning a Song

To transfer good technique from vocalises to songs is a primary goal of singers at all stages of development. Just as practicing should always and without exception begin with concentration on technique in the vocalises, so, then, should careful thought be given to ways of transferring that same technique to songs, whether those songs are classical, theater, or pop. Although there are different types of techniques for various songs, exercises covered in the first year or two of voice study are usually so general that even the most dedicated pop singers will not damage their vocal sound by using them.

The emphasis in transferring technique to songs is not directed, necessarily, toward allowing the singer finally to sound "natural." The emphasis is rather on vocal health, beauty of tone, and effective musical interpretation. Singing "naturally" is almost never good enough. Performers whose techniques give that illusion have generally spent thousands of solitary hours thinking and practicing to improve their performance.

The frequent impression of new voice students is that the incorporation of technique into their songs gives them too much of an operatic sound. Another impression often mentioned is that a song is too high. Because we usually speak with the mouth nearly closed, it seems strange to open it for a more sonorous tone when singing. This fuller sound, which is often thought of by the new student as "too classical," is actually the first step toward beautiful singing and can be heard in good performers working in all styles.

It is also a source of amazement to many to hear themselves producing greater volume and singing on a higher pitch or with a different quality than that to which they have been accustomed all their lives. Learning to sing songs that at first seem too high develops greater breath control and strengthens the vocal muscles. It extends the singer's options when selecting material to perform, enlarges the possibilities for styling, and, quite basically, improves the entire range of the voice.

As with practicing vocalises, the tape recorder is an indispensable aid to learning a song. The singer may have the melody line first taped without, then with, the piano accompaniment, in order to expedite the learning process. As the learning of the song progresses, the singing should periodically be recorded, played back, and carefully analyzed. The teacher's guidance in assessing the technique used in the song and its interpretation is vital, since it is extremely difficult for singers to evaluate themselves. But it is the students who will ultimately decide the extent of their own success. As with vocalizing, the successful singer will be the one who follows directions given, in the most minute detail, and who practices consistently with enormous concentration.

The order of the steps for learning a song varies according to the learning patterns of a singer. The following approach is but one workable method. To help illustrate the steps, an art song from the anthology, "Beneath a Weeping Willow's Shade," will be used. The assumption is made that any song studied has been approved for the student's use by the teacher.

To begin, record the melody on the tape recorder, first without the accompaniment, then with the complete piano part. Play the recording of the unaccompanied melody through once, then repeat if desired, silently following along with the music.

Next, play the melody with accompaniment. Notice the general feeling of the music, whether, for example, it is heavy or lilting, joyous or subdued, or descriptive (with an accent every two beats, like a march, or every three beats like a waltz). Check the dates of the composer to find out if the song is fairly recent or from some other period. By considering the text and music, determine the overall style of the song. Was it intended to be a folk song, a song for worship, for the theater, or for some other use entirely?

"Beneath a Weeping Willow's Shade" (see Exercise 4.1) was written during the lifetime of George Washington; therefore, the picture of men and women in the dress of that time dancing to the music of the harpsichord might readily be imagined. The feeling is light and buoyant, with an accent on every third beat.

Rewind the tape to the unaccompanied melody and, using the syllable *la,* sing along, being careful that the sung

Beneath a Weeping Willow's Shade

Piano acc.
adapted from
the original by
Roy S. Stoughton

**Dedicated to George
Washington, Esquire**

Words and
Music by
Francis Hopkinson
(1737–1791)

heart she laid, And plain-tive was her moan, And plain-tive was her moan.
dieu," she cried, "I ne'er shall see thee more, I ne'er shall see thee more."

The mock-bird sat up-on a bough, The

mock-bird sat up-on a bough And lis-ten'd to her lay, Then

to the dis - tant hills he bore The dul - cet notes a - way, Then

to the dis - tant hills he bore The dul - cet notes a - way, The

dul - cet notes a - way, The dul - cet notes a - way. way.

pitches and rhythms are exactly the same as those heard on the piano. This step should be repeated as many times as necessary to accomplish this goal. One time-saving device is to isolate those places in the melody that are repeatedly sung incorrectly or are in any way difficult. Above them, mark an *x* with pencil which can later be erased as they are mastered. In "Beneath a Weeping Willow's Shade," measures 8, 9, and 35 might provoke confusion because of the dotted rhythms (notes with dots following are held half again longer than they would be normally, resulting in the shortening of the note that follows). Measures 25 and 26 might prove surprising because of the introduction of wider intervals between the notes of the melody (until that point, most of the notes have been adjacent to one another in the scale, or very nearly so).

When the pitches and rhythms are learned, whisper the words of the text in rhythm while playing back the unaccompanied melody. This could well be done two or three times, or until there are no difficulties performing this step. In all songs, the syllable is found directly underneath the note to which it corresponds. Frequently, two or more notes are sung on the same syllable. In measure 8, "wil-" is sung on two notes, and in measure 32 "way" is sung on seven notes.

After the music and text have been put together, some time should be taken to analyze and picture the meaning and mood of the text. Read the text aloud. What exactly is the text trying to communicate? Then, with pencil, mark a comma in each place where a breath seems sensible, taking into consideration the sound of the melody and the meaning of the words. Breaths are taken to separate thoughts. For example, in measure 12, a breath separates "Her hand upon her heart she laid" from "And plaintive was her moan." And in measure 4, second verse, a breath separates "Fond Echo to her strains replied" from "The winds her sorrow bore." Sections of repeated text, such as those found in measure 28, are also separated with a breath.

Another necessity, in order to effectively give expression to a text, is to research the meaning of any words not understood. In "Beneath a Weeping Willow's Shade," measure 3, second verse, Echo (the nymph from Greek mythology who faded away for love of Narcissus, retaining only her voice) is mentioned. And in measure 27, the word *dulcet* (meaning "melodious") is used. In foreign-language songs, every word must be clearly understood by the singer, a process that is simplified as more and more foreign-language songs are learned. Knowing the "general meaning" is never enough.

After the music and text are memorized, attention should be turned once again to technique and its transference to the song. The correctness of the breathing should be checked. Are the abdominals moving out at inhalation? Are the ribs maintained in an upward and outward position? Are the shoulders still and in the proper position?

And what about good articulation?

Strange as it feels, the essence of good articulation is to sing with the upper and lower teeth apart, using a flexible tongue and lips to form the words. This combination coupled with a constantly elevated soft palate allows for more vertical space inside the mouth, which prevents the sound from being unduly dampened by its soft structures.

Depending on the type of tone quality a teacher might prefer, one abbreviated pronunciation guide for new students might be the following:

Vernacular	International Phonetic Alphabet	Guide
ee	[i]	Pronounced as the vowel sound in "feet," using low jaw, high palate, tongue and lips forward.
ay	[e]	A diphthong which begins like the vowel sound in "pet" and, at its release, concludes in the position for an *ih,* as in "it," with no movement of the lowered jaw between sounds.
ah	[a]	The vowel in "palm," with the same low jaw position used for *ee and ay.*
oh	[o]	The position of the palate for this sound is high. Heard in "tone," this sound uses a jaw position that is somewhat lower than for the preceding vowels with the palate raised.
oo	[u]	The vowel sound heard in "moon," pronounced with lips forward and the jaw in the low position used for *oh.* The palate will be as highly arched as possible.

Vowels should be modified from the foregoing guide in words that require it, so that pronunciation of texts is perceived as natural. For example, the vowel in the first syllable of "willow" will be pronounced in a way that more closely resembles its spoken pronunciation than it does "*wee*llow."

In good articulation, a tone quality should be continuous throughout the phrase. This means that the character of the tone should not fluctuate between shrill and hooty as syllables change.

Consonants, because they dissipate more rapidly than vowels, must be emphasized more heavily in singing than in speech. Otherwise, the meaning of a text will be totally lost even in a small auditorium.

When a song has been thoroughly worked through, first musically, then technically, it is time to consider how to communicate it. To be videotaped is a great help when working to improve this area. Practicing before a full-length mirror is a useful alternative. The singer needs, quite literally, to picture the things being sung about. Concentration, which must also be practiced, is the key. Songs must be delivered with great energy to an audience. New singers often feel they are almost yelling when they are singing at a volume level acceptable to a teacher. To effectively convince an audience takes double or triple the amount of energy one would imagine. If a student occasionally overdoes it, the teacher will be the first to say so. Even through piano introductions and interludes, the singer's thoughts must center on the mood and content of the song. If one lapses, even momentarily, dramatic intensity will be lost. In the beginning stages, when the transference of technique is often awkward, it is frequently difficult to maintain energy and concentration. But in time, these will come, enabling a singer actually to "sell" a song.

Sample Song-Learning Method

Record melody, first with, then without, accompaniment. Develop familiarity with both versions.

Define the historical period, mood, and type of song.

Sing along with unaccompanied melody using the syllable *la,* marking difficult places with an *x.* Practice until rhythm and pitches are absolutely accurate.

Whisper the words of the text in rhythm while listening to the unaccompanied melody.

Sing text and pitches with unaccompanied melody until learned securely. Sing with accompanied melody.

Read the text aloud and analyze its meaning.

With commas, mark in appropriate breaths. Circle expression markings.

Concentrate on the use of good vocal technique in the song.

Using a tape recorder, review articulation.

Practice "selling" the song by picturing its text and performing it with great and consistent energy.

When applying this method to a song in a style different from that of an art song—for example, "Send In the Clowns" from the musical theater idiom—exactly the same procedure can be used. The biggest difference will be in the mood and styling of the song. The mood of "Beneath a Weeping Willow's Shade," composed in the eighteenth century, is mournful, and intended for private, rather than highly commercial, entertainment. Vocally, an eighteenth-century art song is performed in a very prescribed manner, with continuous vibrato and carefully defined dynamics, which must be meticulously observed.

"Send In the Clowns," on the other hand, was composed fairly recently, with a reflective text, and is part of a larger musical theater work, *A Little Night Music*. In musical theater pieces, the singer has an opportunity for more variety of styling, as long as what one does is closely related to the composer's indications in the music. Often, the singing will be more speechlike, meaning that more "straight" tone, using little or no vibrato, is employed. To intelligently interpret a musical theater song or operatic aria, the entire story and other music from the show or opera must be studied, in order to understand how the character might sing the song. This is done by borrowing recordings and scores from the library.

A folk song, such as "The Riddle Song" (see p. 93), may be from anywhere and any period. This song is from England, its original date of composition unknown. It is quietly clever, and is most attractive when sung with almost continuous vibrato. Because of their casual nature and because frequently they have not been transcribed, most folk songs have been reworked countless times. The folk song can be sung with any vocal quality necessary to communicate the spirit of its text, from lyrical to bawdy. The singer should have a consistent enough vocal technique that vocal effects for folk songs, dynamic in presentation and harmless to the voice, can be consciously devised. This same ideal should be the ultimate goal of singers in all types of vocal music performance.

5 Basic Principles of Vocal Technique

In order to explain more completely the reasoning behind the singing process, some additional information, particularly that related to articulation and acoustics, will be given in this chapter. While much of the information is based on scientific research, some is based on pedagogical experience, a combination of sources common to all teachers. When a process is thoroughly understood, its outcome tends to be more effective, and therefore meaningful. Undesirable effects can be analyzed and avoided, while desirable ones can be incorporated and utilized.

Ideas about articulation vary greatly from teacher to teacher. At one end of the spectrum are those who ask the students for an extremely pulled-down larynx and a deep yawning quality in the tone. At the other are those who speak often of closing the mouth and lifting the muscles in the upper part of the cheeks for a smiling, bright quality. Because the tone quality a teacher elects to teach is so evidently a matter of personal choice, it is important that students be aware of the options open to them when they are in the process of selecting an instructor.

Taking some elements from both extremes of the spectrum can produce a method of articulation that is vocally comfortable and healthy and clearly understandable to listeners.

As the singer begins to transfer technique to songs, it

is important to realize that, as one maintains the jaw in a slightly lowered position, so that upper and lower teeth can be kept apart, the throat should be kept open, as it was for the vocalises. The stretching open of the throat might feel exaggerated at first, but it should not feel uncomfortable. Both a throat that is too closed and one that is too widely stretched will produce a feeling of tension in the front of the neck just under the lower jaw. It is imperative to sing with a relaxed neck, since constricting its muscles, in front or back, can pull the cartilages of the larynx into positions that will put unnecessary strain on the vocal cords. Singing with a tight neck is one of the major problems with which beginning voice students must be concerned. It distorts articulation, impairs quality, and markedly limits the number of pitches that can be sung. Often, its most obvious manifestation is a sore throat.

Working from the inside out, when the singer begins to concentrate on opening the throat, a phenomenon similar to yawning, it will be noticed that several things happen. Most obviously, the jaw drops, giving a stretching feeling to the chewing muscles. Simultaneously, the soft palate arches and the tongue lowers. These characteristics should always be maintained while singing a song. A tight jaw or tongue that is too high or too far forward will render articulation less distinguishable, by introducing the *uh* vowel into words intended to project an *ah* sound. Since the soft palate also serves as the floor of the nasal cavity, a lowered soft palate will contribute to the production of a tone with nasal quality. (The slight amount of nasality previously suggested for the extreme high and low pitches of the vocalises will not be counterproductive.) Another important function of the raised palate is that, because of its firm surface, it appears to promote clarity, or give "focus," to the tone. A combination of arched palate and accelerated airflow greatly enhances a tone's carrying power.

Working from the outside inward, when the singer elevates the muscles in the upper part of the cheeks, the upper lip is raised, thus exposing more of the hard surfaces of the teeth. This will contribute to the production of brilliant tone, but it should not be substituted for energetic airflow and arched palate. Because the upper cheeks are elevated, it does not stand to reason that a broad smile should necessarily result. If the text indicates that such an expression would be appropriate, the singer should follow that suggestion. But often a text will imply a more serious expression, for which the lips should be more relaxed.

As singers inhale, they prepare mentally for what they are about to sing. They think of the syllable they will be producing, and thereby assist in the physical, as well as mental, preparation of the body for that syllable.

The *attack,* or beginning of the tone, should feel comfortable and should be neither too explosive nor too breathy. In an explosive attack, the airstream forces the vocal cords apart, and they slap back together again with more force than is vocally healthy or audibly pleasing. In that instance, a popping sound will precede the syllable. In a breathy attack, when a slight rush of air precedes or accompanies the syllable, the cords do not close firmly enough, and air, which could be more efficiently used, is wasted. Consequently, if a singer makes an explosive attack, it is necessary to relax the neck muscles and slow the rate at which one is contracting the abdominals and blowing air. If the attack is breathy, the airflow needs to be accelerated, by pulling in more rapidly on the abdominals and blowing harder.

Smoking is another common cause of breathy production. In the person who smokes, the membranes covering the cords are filled with fluid. Instead of healthy cords opening and closing hundreds of times per second to release clearly defined vibrations, the fluid-filled membranes approximate each other with a closure that is anything but firm. If smoking is stopped, there should be a marked improvement in the clarity of the voice within two weeks.

Following an efficient inhalation and attack, the singer thinks of the totality of the line being sung. To avoid a choppy, word-by-word interpretation of the text, one needs to concentrate on sustaining the vowels of each syllable for as long as it is rhythmically correct to do so. This aids greatly in the singing of a *legato,* or smooth, line, one of the prime objectives of advanced singers.

The following are some of the most basic points of correct articulation with which the singer should be familiar:

For the sake of tone quality, the *uh* and *ow* sounds are always altered to an *ah.* This practice is applicable to such words as "love," "the," and "down." Modification of this basic vowel should be used when needed, especially for diphthongs.

Vowels should be clear and brilliant. *Ee,* as in "see," *eh,* as in "when," and *ay* as in "say," are all pronounced as an *ee,* with lowered jaw and using only the slightest modification.

When *diphthongs,* compound vowels, are sung, the first sound is sustained, with the second sound added at the release of the syllable. For example, in the *a* of "shade," the opening vowel sound *eh* (e) is the sustained sound. The *a* concludes with an *ih* (i) sound, which is added immediately preceding the *d* of "shade" (e.g., sheh-ihd). Some other common diphthongs are heard in the words "eye," "poi," and the aforementioned "down," in which the sustained *ah* (a) sound concludes on an *oo* (u).

Consonants are always formed using the tongue and lips, with space between the upper and lower teeth.

When two or more notes are sung on the same syllable, the singer should slide between them. Articulating each of the notes with an *h*, a very common approach, requires that, for each *h*, the airflow be stopped. This, in turn, interrupts the legato line. (Sliding on a run differs from scooping up to a pitch on an attack, which should be avoided.)

The addition of an extra syllable to the end of a word, such as "friend-*uh*," is indicative of overemphasis, and should be avoided.

Linking the final consonant of one word to the initial sound of the following word, when it changes the meaning of the text, should be avoided. An often-cited example of this is, "I'm old."

Good articulation should leave the neck free from tension and be unobtrusive yet render a text clearly understandable.

The measure of effective articulation lies in the quality of its perception. If words cannot be heard, or if their clear comprehension is difficult for an audience, much of the emotional and intellectual impact of the song is lost. For that reason, some basic information concerning *acoustics,* the study of sound, will be presented.

As the highly flexible vocal cords stretch across the top of the trachea, they open and close in a wavelike motion, from bottom to top. This action divides the exhaled airstream into numerous tiny puffs, or wave fronts, every second. If, for example, they open and close 440 times in a second, the buzz they produce will be perceived as the first A above middle C.

As the wave fronts are emitted, billions of molecules of air are pushed outward in all directions from the source. The moving molecules do not experience a permanent displacement; after the wave passes by, they return to their original position (see Figure 5.1). The moving outward of the molecules is termed *compression,* and the return of the molecules to their original position is called *rarefaction.*

Sound travels at the rate of approximately eleven hundred feet (335 m.) per second. It enters the outer ear and travels through the tubular canal, which is approximately one inch (25 mm.) long. At the end of the ear canal is the sensitive membranous *eardrum,* which vibrates at the same frequency with which it is disturbed by the compressed air molecules (see Figure 5.2).

The motion of the eardrum activates three small bones

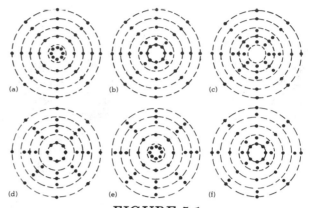

FIGURE 5.1
Traveling pattern of
sound waves through air

called *ossicles,* which are suspended in the *middle ear*—a cavity in the skull. Their movement sets up a vibration in the *oval window,* an oval membrane in the wall of the cochlea. The *cochlea,* a spiral bone in the *inner ear,* is filled with fluid. Nerve endings, which transmit vibrating movement to the brain, are also found in the cochlea.

Resonance is a response to a produced sound, during which that sound is prolonged and intensified. The three primary resonators for the voice are, in order of importance, the throat, the mouth, and the nose. Research has shown that, although a singer might feel sympathetic vibrations in the chest, trachea, larynx, or sinuses, those areas have little or no value as resonators. When the surfaces of the resonators are stretched to form a yawn or open throat, they are hardened, thereby conducting sound more effectively. The resonators also filter out, or dampen, some sounds, a

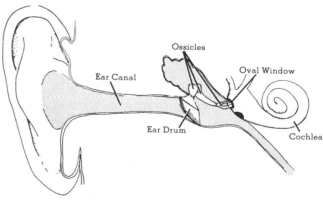

FIGURE 5.2
The ear

process that is even more evident when their surfaces are flaccid.

It should be noted that the nose is an occasional resonator, while the throat and mouth function constantly as resonators. Nasal resonance is primarily necessary for the production of nasal consonants, such as *m, n,* and *ng.* It is also important in the singing of foreign languages, notably French, because of their nasal vowels.

The shape of the primary resonators determines, to a large extent, the quality of tone produced. When the singer wishes to communicate a vowel, it is usually sustained as long as is rhythmically possible, since a vowel can be projected far better than a consonant. This is because the movement in the sound wave of a vowel, categorized a "tone," is even or repetitive and, by nature, has a longer duration. In contrast, although there are a few exceptions, such as *m* and *n*, most consonants fall into the acoustic category of "noise," which is characterized by uneven or nonrepetitive, sound waves (see Figure 5.3). The properties of these types of waves cause their vibrations to fall off quickly, creating a need for high-energy pronunciation of these kinds of sounds.

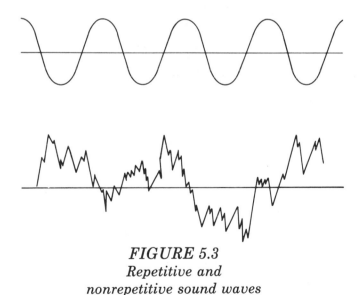

FIGURE 5.3
Repetitive and
nonrepetitive sound waves

Another area of acoustics that is of particular interest to singers is registration. *Registers* have been defined as "a series of consecutive similar vocal tones which the musically trained ear can differentiate at specific places from another adjoining series of likewise internally similar tones."*

Pitch-wise, registers are often referred to by beginning

*M. Nadoleczny, *Untersuchungen über den Kunstgesang* (Berlin: Springer, 1923).

singing students as "low voice," "regular voice," or "high voice." In terms of volume, they are sometimes differentiated by the terms "heavy voice" and "light voice." Regardless of the names applied to registers, most teachers would probably agree that the goal of the student should be to eliminate awareness of their existence. If a singer has "breaks" in the voice and changes in tone quality (vowel color) between high and low pitches, it is simply because that student has not yet learned to coordinate airflow with the actions of the laryngeal musculature and resonators.

Generally, researchers refer to three main registers: *chest, middle,* and *head* in the female voice, and *chest, head,* and *falsetto* in the male voice. In the trained voice, each register is about an octave in length, with several notes that can be sung in either register at those points where the registers overlap (see Figure 5.4).

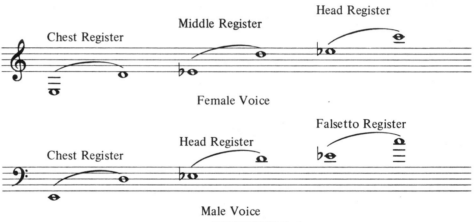

FIGURE 5.4
*Approximate registers
of the singing voice*

In nearly all untrained singers, one of the registers, frequently chest, will be used considerably more than the others. It is the task of the student to practice exercising the voice throughout its entire range, so that songs might be interpreted with greater style and beauty.

In those areas where registers overlap, the register is used that makes the most dramatic or musical sense. For example, when a soprano sings "Beneath a Weeping Willow's Shade" (Example 5.1), the word "alone" in measures 5 and 6 could technically be sung in either chest or middle register, but since the text surrounding it is sung in middle register, it is desirable to utilize the same for this word.

EXAMPLE 5.1

6 The Theatrics of Singing

The ultimate goal of most singers is to share their music, either as a member of a group or as a soloist. The conductor or director of a group explains its style of presentation to performers, but solo singers must choose their own.

Most singers, when they first begin to perform, are extremely nervous. Frankly, in fact, it can be counted on. But as one performs more, there is an increase in the ease and effectiveness with which one sings. Singers, unlike instrumentalists, do not express themselves through an object apart from their person. They open up their being to success and failure. Regardless of circumstances, committed singers keep working and sharing. Focusing intense concentration upon giving to the audience often helps channel the increased energy felt in the preperformance hours.

To become a magnetic singing performer, which is, after all, the ultimate goal, it is highly advisable to integrate into one's study, work in piano, acting, and movement (fencing, dance, and so on). The contributions of all of these to a high-quality performance in every style of singing, from pop to opera, are enormous. These disciplines need not be studied exhaustively—even two years' work in each would be helpful—but the importance of their integration into one's preparation for performance cannot be overestimated.

The study of piano is important because of the basic musical knowledge it can afford. It is essential for intelligent communication with accompanists, or with a conductor in a group situation. If students periodically hum along with music they are playing during their practice sessions, a facility in sight reading will often develop rapidly. In addition, much will be learned about basic musical terminology concerning volume levels and expression markings.

Studying acting is helpful because one can learn to project and to concentrate, to think thoughts appropriate to a given character or situation. And to honestly interpret a song, it is important to master the technique of having thoughts logically connected to the song, not only while conveying the text, but also during instrumental introductions, interludes, and conclusions. For example, during an instrumental introduction, singers should not contemplate the temperature of the room or the possible reactions to their performance. Instead, if one is singing "Beneath a Weeping Willow's Shade," the singer might picture a girl in eighteenth-century dress, sitting under a willow, despairing over the departure of her loved one. The dominant attitude the performer might adopt for this song—and one must always be adopted—might be compassion. This attitude, and visualization of the pictures and thoughts of the text, must be maintained, without interruption, until the conclusion of the song.

In addition, acting, which, like singing, is a learned technique, will introduce the singer to various ways of using the body to communicate ideas and feelings. This is another critical aspect of effective presentation of all styles. "Feeling it," without training in the specifics and effects of movement, is, like singing naturally, almost never good enough. Courses in acting fundamentals and programs integrating voice, acting, and dance, such as music theatre or opera workshops, are absolutely essential for a singer of any style of music.

Like acting, movement, and specifically dance, gives performers an awareness of the picture they are making onstage, and will teach them to project energetically to an audience. From ballet to jazz, much can be learned from posture and stance, even of the impact caused by the smallest gesture. Fencing is helpful for male singers, particularly in the area of operatic singing.

Broadly speaking, there are three general categories or styles of singing, as noted earlier. They are classical, popular, and theater. For the sake of versatility, a performer will sometimes cross over from one category to another. But the general practice is that one of the styles will usually be of considerably greater appeal to a singer than the other two, and in that one the performer will specialize. Songs in the anthology in this volume are taken from all three areas. Because the manner of presentation for every style varies considerably, a brief overview of each will be given.

Classical singing, which includes opera, oratorio, and recital, as well as most "legitimate" music for the church, demands, by tradition, that a great deal be communicated with practically no stage movement. As in the other areas, much can be communicated by stance. If the song is prayerful, it might well be sung with the feet placed more closely together. If the song is assertive, the feet might be planted firmly apart. The singer might lean slightly forward if the character of the song is telling a story, particularly in an excited or earnest manner. One might lean backward if the song conveys a passive or depressed text. The singer seldom, if ever, takes a step during the song. In a recital setting, the singer might choose to stand close to the piano, in its curve, while singing something of an intimate nature, such as a lullaby; and somewhat in front of it for an assertive song, such as a sea chanty.

The visual focus in all styles of singing is determined by the text of the song. A narrative song, such as "When Love Is Kind" (see the anthology), will be sung looking directly at the audience (periodically changing the place of focus, in accordance with the music). "Greensleeves," because of its text, might be sung looking at the imagined love, until "Greensleeves was all my joy . . . ," where the focus might be shifted more directly to the audience, to better emphasize the final words of the text.

Songs of the classical type, called *art songs,* are performed exactly as the composer wrote them. With the exception of contemporary music, there is usually no extemporaneous styling. Spontaneous expression, a vital part of all performances, must fit well within the dictates of the composer's score. Classical singers must also prepare songs and arias in several languages besides English—notably, Italian, French, and German.

Since performances of classical music are usually not electronically amplified, the classical singer is trained to sing without benefit of a microphone, which is good discipline for theater and pop singers also.

Dress for the classical singer is usually formal. Suits or tuxedos for men are the norm, with long dresses for women. Solid-colored dresses with long sleeves are slimming and will focus attention on the singer's face. Prints on a dress fabric are often distracting. Basic rules for good dressing apply to onstage performance as well. Numerous books are available on the subject.

Audiences frequently pass abiding judgment on a performer during the first minute onstage. Because of that, and because an entrance can be used to help set a mood for a program, it should be worked through carefully and practiced many times. When it is time to go onstage, the singer should locate a spot to stand where the lights will show the performer to best advantage. Then one should walk confidently to that predetermined spot, looking straight ahead all the while. It is important never to look down, since a lowered gaze can signify confusion or discomfort to an audience. For a smooth walk, the abdominals should be contracted, as in dance, and the arms should move in opposition to the feet. As the singer faces the audience, during both entrances and bows, friendliness and an enormous desire to communicate must be projected.

Popular singing currently includes many styles, such as folk, country, jazz, and rock. In pop singing, the emphasis is on individuality, both in dress and presentation. The performer in this style of music is encouraged to be "packaged" as uniquely as possible. Dress is determined, very often, by the type of picture the performer wishes to present to enhance the style of music being sung. One might wear jeans to give a "country" feeling, or, for avant-garde rockers, an unusual costume design in a shiny or extraordinary fabric might be appropriate.

Stage movement for the pop singer might run the gamut from that described for the classical singer to a highly frenzied, and carefully choreographed, dance routine.

Good microphone technique is a must. "Paging" the mike, the moving of the cord back in the direction of the amplifier while holding the mike in the opposite hand, requires considerable practice. Also, much experimentation is necessary to figure out the proper distance from the singer's mouth to the microphone, in order to ensure the desired vocal effect. For more "presence," intensified contact, in a song of an intimate nature, the microphone will be held close to the singer. For high or loud tones, the distance will be greater.

To secure a club date, the pop singer needs to have thoroughly prepared in excess of forty songs of various types, which are divided into groups, or *sets*. Sets, each containing approximately six songs, can be assembled using different strategies. One basic pattern might resemble the following:

Opener	positive text, up-tempo
Credibility Song	sincere lyrics, slower than the Opener
Slow Song	
Song of Choice	new or unfamiliar
False Ending	dramatic, up-tempo
Encore	more subdued than the False Ending, meaningful for the audience

Sets must be assembled with careful thought to the overall effect of the various styles, harmonies, and lyrics.

Pop songs are usually learned from *lead sheets* (see Figure 6.1), on which only the melody line is given and the letter names for chords indicated. That is, no specific notes are

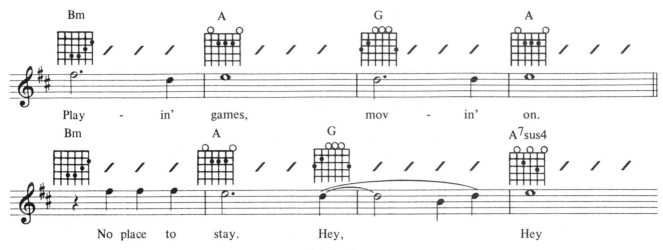

FIGURE 6.1
Excerpt from lead sheet

indicated for the accompaniment, so that instrumentalists are free to improvise. Unlike classical and theater singing, the performance of popular songs in transposed keys, either higher or lower than they were originally written, is not only acceptable, but expected. Original arrangements of a song, which often completely change its mood, are highly desirable, as long as the new arrangements relate well to the lyrics or the environment of the performance.

Since, at the moment, the commercial sound that is selling best often calls for men to sing in the head and falsetto registers and women to sing primarily in the chest and middle registers, pop singers will frequently sing higher or lower than they would if they were doing classical or theater singing. But because singers should vocalize over at least a three-octave range, this adjustment in ranges should be comfortable if all other aspects of good vocal production are heeded. If vocal difficulties arise from an attempt to sing a song, the pitches of the melody can be modified to accommodate the performer.

Owing to its origins, the category of singing most influenced by the theater is musical theater. The ability to "project" dramatically frequently precedes most musical considerations, especially in the early training of new musical theater performers. "Belting," a style of singing done at a loud volume level in which the chest register is used to its uppermost limits, is taught as a quick way to add energy to a singing performance. Although it is absolutely necessary to belt in order to effectively portray many characters in a musical theater production, ultimately this technique is far from being desirable in terms of vocal health. As with any style of extreme vocal production, it should be carefully monitored. On the other hand, the idea of portraying a rough-spoken character using only dialogue, and reverting to a refined style of singing for that person's songs, is totally incongruous. It is extremely important that theater students take great pains to develop an excellent singing technique, so that they can use voice types suitable to different types of characters. They need to be aware of the potential vocal hazards that might occur, and know how to create their roles in a vocally healthy manner. Hoarseness, often heard among actors, is not an indication of vocal health and can be avoided.

"Selling" the song, as with all types of singing, is the fundamental goal. Specifically, "selling" refers to dramatic components, including energy level, concentration, and characterization. For the successful musical theater performer, all these must be present to the greatest extent possible. Although stage and/or body microphones are almost always used for theater productions, enormous energy must emanate from the actors themselves.

For musical theater auditions, songs are sung only in the original keys and by performers for whom they are appropriate. (Some of the theater songs in the anthology have been transposed for convenience in class use.) For example, a man's song is never sung by a woman, using modified lyrics. A director will usually indicate whether songs are to be sung from the show being cast or from other shows. Failure to pay attention to the director's request indicates laziness and insufficient interest in the show and frequently eliminates a performer from consideration. Again, selling a "package" is of the utmost importance. The auditioner should always be familiar with the proposed show and try to look, sing, and act similar to, but not exactly like, the character one hopes to play. An attempt to identify totally with a character might well work to the auditioner's disadvantage, since the director often has strong preconceived ideas about characterizations and needs to feel an actor is willing to be flexible enough to create the role as the director sees fit. It is important to inquire about the director's preferences.

Because performers for musical theater auditions must often dance as well as read and sing, they must come dressed ready to move. They should be well-groomed, with the hair back from the face, and should look nicely dressed. Stylish jeans and a T-shirt or a leotard with a wraparound skirt is often the most appropriate apparel.

As the discussion of the three categories of singing has proceeded, it has been seen that, although there are major differences between them, they have much in common.

A sense of appreciation for performers in all styles is certainly in order. As singers first begin to perform, it cannot be expected that the proficiency they have attained during private practice will be retained in performance. To learn to concentrate and communicate in performance takes persistent effort. Gradually however, singers will notice—with pleasure—that they are becoming more skilled and effective before an audience.

And pleasure, after all, is what music is all about.

Music Reading 7

It happens often that while searching for music, singers will find a song that they have heard only once or twice. They like the text as well as the music, but cannot remember exactly how the melody moves. Choir members sometimes have parts they wish they could learn prior to a rehearsal. A pianist is not always available, and for that reason, it is highly advisable to develop some ability to read music.

One of the fastest ways to learn this skill, which is really not difficult and only takes practice, is to enroll in a beginning piano or music reading class. As a brief introduction, here is a summary of some of the basic facts.

All traditional music is written on a five-line structure called a staff.

Commonly, higher pitches are indicated in the G clef, or *treble clef,*

while low pitches are shown in the F clef, or *bass clef.*

The most frequently sung pitches are drawn on the staffs below (see Figure 7.1). Although both clefs extend beyond these points, the illustration begins at middle C, a note lo-

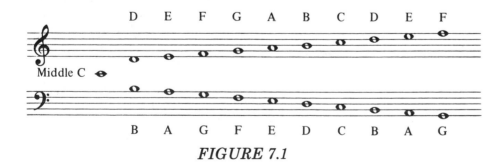

FIGURE 7.1

Notes on Lines 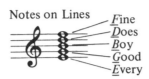 *F*ine
*D*oes
*B*oy
*G*ood
*E*very

Notes on Spaces  E
C
A
F

Treble Clef

Notes on Lines 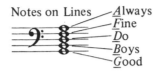 *A*lways
*F*ine
*D*o
*B*oys
*G*ood

Notes in Spaces 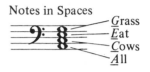 *G*rass
*E*at
*C*ows
*A*ll

Bass Clef

FIGURE 7.2

cated near the insignia above the piano keyboard, at its center.

For years, many people have used mnemonic devices to memorize the letter names of the pitches quickly (for instance, *All Cows Eat Grass*) in which the first letter of each word is the same as a note on the staff (see Figure 7.2). In the case of *All Cows Eat Grass*, the letters correspond to the letter names of the notes located in the spaces (between the staff lines) of the bass clef. *Good Boys Do Fine Always* may be used to help memorize the notes on the lines. These sentences always work from the bottom to the top of the staff. The classic *Every Good Boy Does Fine* assists with learning the notes on the lines in the treble clef, and the letters of the word *FACE* are the same as the notes in the spaces of the treble clef.

At this point, it might be helpful to review the foregoing by identifying the pitches in Exercise 7.1 (the answers are given in inverted type directly below it). For more review, use a beginning piano book.

On the piano keyboard, even easier to memorize than the letter names of notes, one can readily spot the groups of two and three black keys (see the fold-out keyboard in the pocket in the back cover of this book). To the left of a group of two black keys is always a C, and to the right of them, an E. To the left of a group of three black keys is an F, and to the right of them, a B. The keys between the four keys mentioned are arranged in alphabetical order from A to G and simply repeat that pattern.

Using the keyboard and covering its typed letters, practice identifying the white keys until they are thoroughly memorized.

EXERCISE 7.1

At the beginning of a song, the key signature (sharps and flats) is usually indicated. A piano key's sharp (♯) is found immediately to its right, while its flat (♭) is found immediately to its left. A sharp will sound higher than the natural key, while the flat will sound lower. Flats and sharps can be white keys or black keys. The pitches to which the key signature applies can be determined by figuring out the name of the pitch that is located in the same place as the sharp or flat. For example,

indicates a flat on the third line of the treble clef. The note always found on the third line of the treble clef is a B; therefore, the flat indicates a B flat. This means that any B found in the music, even though it may be higher or lower, will be flatted.

Again, using the fold-out keyboard, locate the flats and sharps of all the white keys.

The component of music reading that requires the most practice for many is rhythm. The staff is divided into *mea-*

sures by vertical lines. A *time signature*, at the beginning of a song, consists of two numbers, one above the other. The upper number indicates the number of beats per measure; the lower number shows the type of note that gets one beat. In the time signature $\frac{4}{4}$, the upper 4 shows that there are four beats per measure, while the lower four means that a quarter note gets one beat. In a $\frac{3}{8}$ time signature, there are three beats per measure, and an eighth note gets one beat.

Figure 7.3 lists the most common rhythmic values used in notation. When a dot follows a note, it becomes a half again as long as it would ordinarily be. For example, when a note that gets two beats is followed by a dot, it would then get three beats.

Whole Note	𝅝	= 4 beats
Half Note	𝅗𝅥 or 𝆺	= 2 beats
Quarter Note	𝅘𝅥 or 𝆺	= 1 beat
Eighth Note	𝅘𝅥𝅮 or 𝆺	= ½ beat
Sixteenth Note	𝅘𝅥𝅯 or 𝆺	= ¼ beat

FIGURE 7.3

Practice clapping the rhythms in Exercise 7.2. When they can be clapped without hesitation, recite, or pencil in, the letter names of the pitches to which the rhythms correspond. When the letter names can be recited readily, recite and clap them in rhythm. Next, practice playing the melodies on an actual keyboard. (Melodies for songs may be approached in the same manner.)

EXERCISE 7.2

EXERCISE 7.2 (continued)

Rests, or silences, are designated in a manner similar to that for notes (see Figure 7.4). For example, the whole rest usually gets four beats.

Whole Rest	▬	= 4 beats
Half Rest	▬	= 2 beats
Quarter Rest	𝄽	= 1 beat
Eighth Rest	𝄾	= ½ beat
Sixteenth Rest	𝄿	= ¼ beat

FIGURE 7.4

Play the melody in Exercise 7.3. It should sound familiar.

EXERCISE 7.3

Bibliography

Backus, John. *The Acoustical Foundation of Music.* New York: W. W. Norton & Co., Inc., 1969.

Brodnitz, Friedrich. *Keep Your Voice Healthy* (Second Edition). Waltham, MA: College Hill Press, 1987.

Craig, David. *On Singing Onstage.* New York: Schirmer Books, 1978.

Denes, Peter, and Pinson, Elliot. *The Speech Chain.* Short Hills, NJ: Bell Telephone Laboratories, 1963.

Emmons, Shirlee, and Sonntag, Stanley. *The Art of the Song Recital.* New York: Schirmer Books, 1979.

Fields, Victor Alexander. *Foundations of the Singer's Art.* New York: Vantage Press, 1977.

Gray, Henry. *Anatomy, Descriptive and Surgical.* Philadelphia: Running Press, 1974.

Ladefoged, Peter. *Elements of Acoustic Phonetics.* Chicago: The University of Chicago Press, 1962.

Large, John. *Contributions of Voice Research to Singing.* San Diego: College Hill Press, 1980.

Large, John. *Vocal Registers in Singing.* Paris: Mouton, 1973.

McGaw, Charles. *Acting Is Believing.* New York: Holt, Rinehart and Winston, 1966.

Miller, Richard. *The Structure of Singing.* New York: Schirmer Books, 1986.

Novak, Elaine. *Performing in Musicals.* New York: Schirmer Books, 1988.

Saunders, William H. *The Larynx.* Summit, N.J.: CIBA Corporation, 1964.

Silver, Fred. *Auditioning for Musical Theatre.* New York: Newmarket Press, 1985.

Vennard, William. *Developing Voices.* New York: Carl Fischer, Inc., 1973.

Vennard, William. *Singing, the Mechanism and the Technic.* New York: Carl Fischer, Inc., 1969.

Zemlin, Willard. *Speech and Hearing Science.* Englewood Cliffs, N.J.: Prentice-Hall, Inc., 1981.

Part Two: SONG ANTHOLOGY

Folk Songs

Folk Songs

All the Pretty Little Horses

American

Allegretto—with a graceful motion

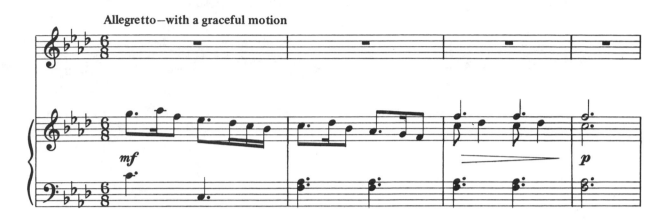

Hush - a - by, don't you cry, Go to sleep - y lit - tle ba - by.

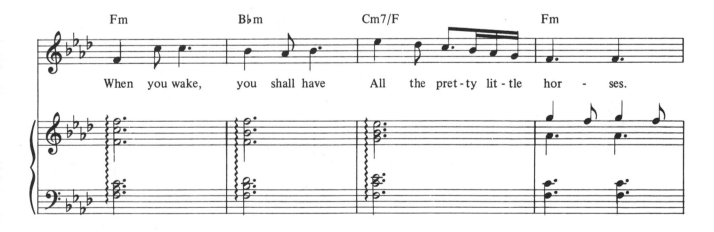

When you wake, you shall have All the pret - ty lit - tle hor - ses.

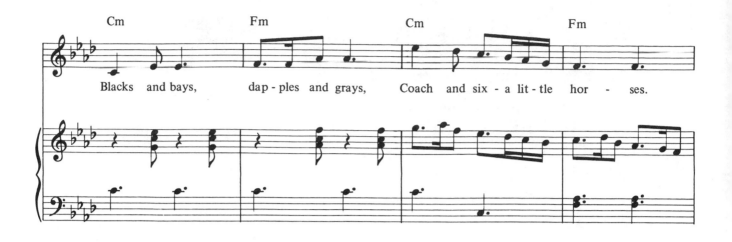

Blacks and bays, dap-ples and grays, Coach and six-a lit-tle hor - ses.

Hush - a - by, don't you cry, Go to sleep -y lit-tle ba — by.

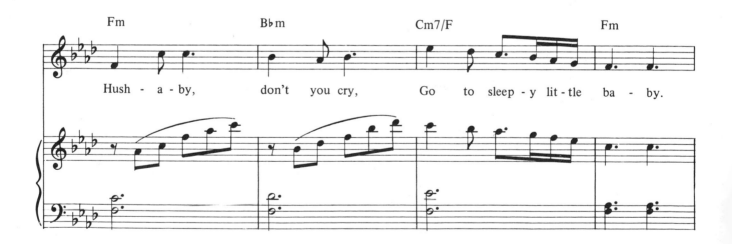

Hush - a - by, don't you cry, Go to sleep -y lit-tle ba — by.

All Through the Night

Welsh

1. Sleep, my love, and peace at-tend thee All through the night; Guard - ian an - gels God will lend thee,

2. Though I roam a min - strel lone - ly, All through the night; My true harp shall praise thee on - ly,

All through the night.
Soft the drow-sy

All through the night.
Love's young dream, a -

hours are creep - ing,
Hill and vale in slum - ber steep - ing,

las! is o - ver,
Yet my strains of love shall ho - ver,

Love a - lone his watch is keep - ing
All through the night.

Near the pres - ence of my lov - er,
All through the night.

59

Amazing Grace

American
Folk Hymn Tune

A -

maz - ing___ grace! how sweet the sound, That
Grace that___ taught my heart to fear, And

saved a___ wretch like___ me! _____ I
grace my___ fears re - lieved; _____ How

once____ was____ lost but now____ am____ found, Was
pre - cious____ did that grace____ ap - pear The

blind, but____ now I see._____ 'Twas
hour I____ first be -

lieved!_____

*Repeat first verse, if desired.

62

The Ash Grove
(High Voice)

Wales

The ash grove, how graceful, how plainly 'tis speaking, the wind through it playing his language for me. When over its branches the sunlight is breaking, a host of kind faces is gazing at

me. The friends of my child-hood a-gain are be-

fore me, each step wakes a mem-'ry as free-ly I roam. With

soft whis-pers lad-en, its leaves rus-tle o'er me; the

ash grove, the ash grove that shel-tered my home. My

out of __ the __ shad - ows their lov - ing __ looks __ greet me, and

wist - ful - ly __ search - ing the leaf - y green dome, I

find oth - er __ fa - ces fond bend - ing __ to __ greet me; the

ash grove, __ the __ ash grove a - lone is my home.

The Ash Grove
(Low Voice)

Wales

Stately

The ash grove how graceful how plainly 'tis speaking, the wind through it playing has language for me, when over its branches the sunlight is breaking, a host of kind faces is gazing at

me. The friends of my child-hood a - gain are be -

fore me, each step wakes a mem-'ry as free-ly I roam. With

soft whis-pers lad - en, its leaves rus - tle o'er me; the

ash grove, the ash grove that shel-tered my home. My

laugh - ter is __ o - ver, my step los - es __ light - ness, old

coun - try - side __ meas - ures steal soft on my ear; I

on - ly re - mem - ber the past and __ its __ bright - ness, the

dear ones __ I __ mourn for a - gain ga - ther here. From __

out of __ the __ shadows their loving looks __ greet me, and wistfully __ searching the leafy green dome; I find other __ faces fond bending __ to greet me; the ash grove, __ the __ ash grove a-lone is my home.

Down by the Salley Gardens

Words by
W.B. Yeats

Irish

*Salley-Willow Tree

gar - dens with __ lit - tle snow white feet. She

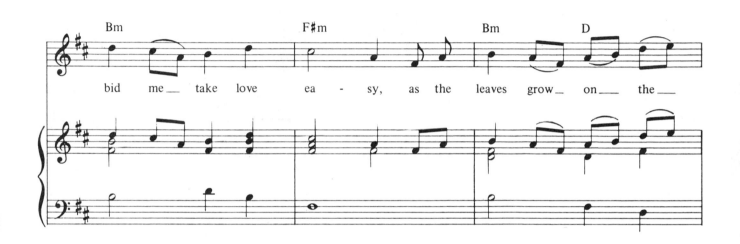

bid me __ take love ea - sy, as the leaves grow __ on __ the __

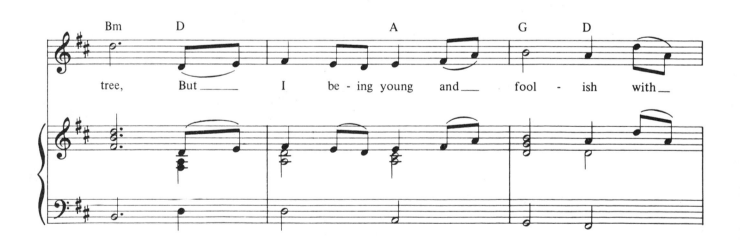

tree, But ____ I be - ing young and __ fool - ish with __

her did ___ not a - gree.

In a field _____ by the ___ riv - er my ___

love and __ I did stand And _____ on my __ lean - ing ___

73

Every Night When the Sun Goes In

Mournfully

American
(Appalachian)

Ev-'ry night when the sun goes in, ev-'ry night when the sun goes in, ev-'ry night when the sun goes in I hang my head and lone-some

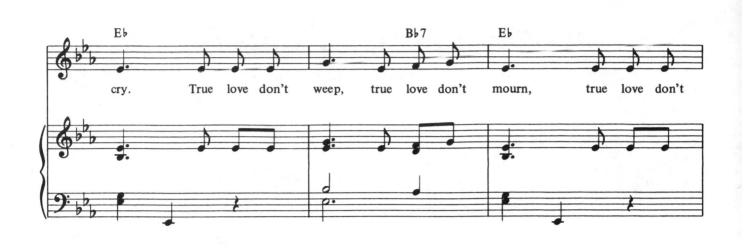

cry. True love don't weep, true love don't mourn, true love don't

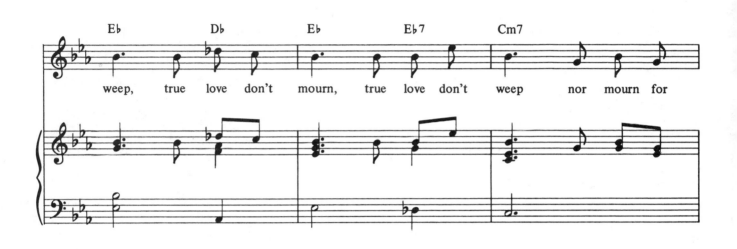

weep, true love don't mourn, true love don't weep nor mourn for

me, I'm goin' a - way to Mar - ble Town.

I wish to the Lord that train would come; I wish to the

Lord that train would come; I wish to the Lord that train would

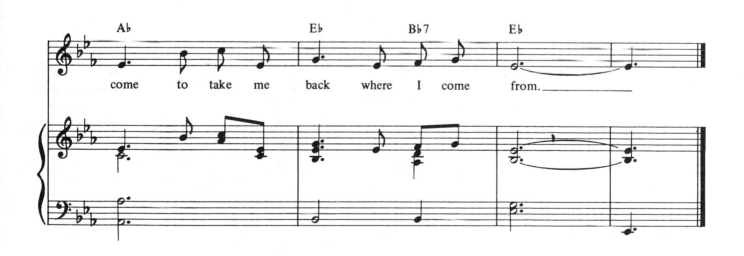

come to take me back where I come from._____

Green Bushes

Ireland

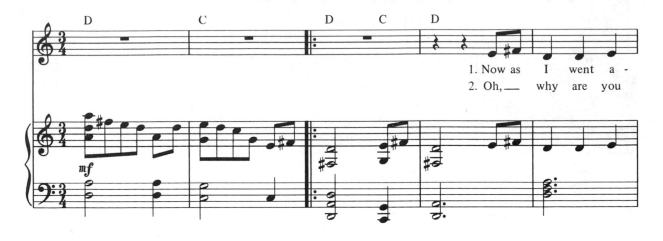

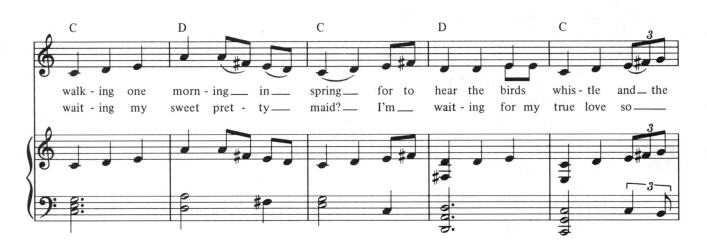

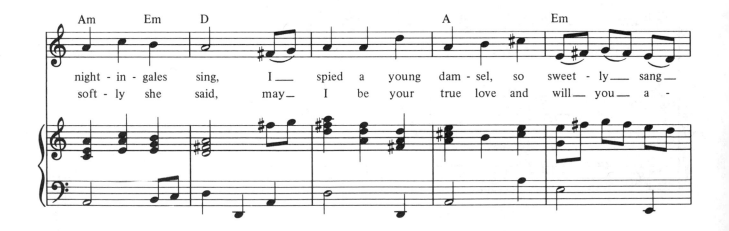

1. Now as I went a-walking one morning in spring for to hear the birds whistle and the nightingales sing, I spied a young damsel, so sweetly sang

2. Oh, why are you waiting my sweet pretty maid? I'm waiting for my true love so softly she said, may I be your true love and will you a-

by those green bush-es where he thinks to __ meet me. And __

when he came there and he saw she was __ gone, __ he __ looked all a-

round him like __ a man quite for - lorn. She's __ gone with some oth - er, she's false __ un - to __

me __ so fare - well to green bush-es for - e - ver, __ said he.

Greensleeves
(High Voice)

1. A - las, my love, ye do me wrong, to
2. have been read - y at your hand, to

cast me off dis - cour - teous - ly, And I have loved
grant what - ev - er you would crave, I have both waged

you so long,_ de - light - ing in _ your com - pa - ny.
life and land,_ your love _ and good - will for to have.

Green - sleeves_ was all my joy, _____ Green - sleeves_ was my de - light,

Green - sleeves was my heart of gold,_ and who but my La - dy Green - sleeves? I

2nd time—Rit.

1st time

2nd time

2nd time—Rit.

Greensleeves
(Low Voice)

1. A - las, my love, ye do me wrong, to
2. have been read - y at your hand, to

cast me off dis - cour - teous - ly, And I have loved
grant what - ev - er you would crave, I have both waged

The Gypsy Rover

British

1. The
2. She

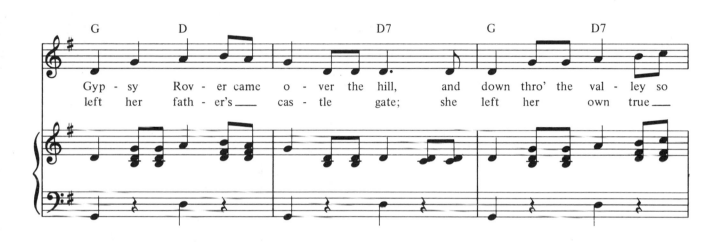

Gyp - sy Rov - er came o - ver the hill, and down thro' the val - ley so
left her fath - er's ___ cas - tle gate; she left her own true ___

shad - y. He whist - led and he sang till the green woods rang and he
lov - er; she left her ser - vants ___ and es - tate to ___

won the heart of a la - - - dy.
fol - low the Gyp - sy___ Rov - - - er.

Ah dee doo, ah dee do da day. Ah dee do, ah dee day dee. He

whist-led and he sang till the green woods rang, and he won the heart of a

la - - dy.

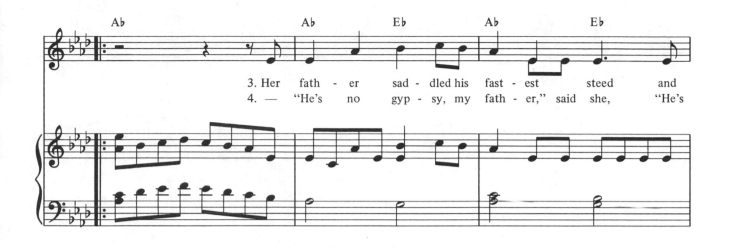

3. Her fath - er sad - dled his fast - est steed and
4. — "He's no gyp - sy, my fath - er," said she, "He's

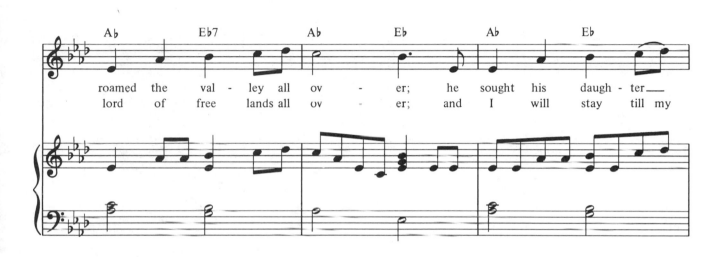

roamed the val - ley all ov - er; he sought his daugh - ter___
lord of free lands all ov - er; and I will stay till my

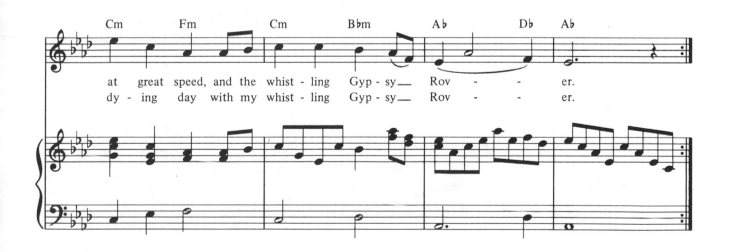

at great speed, and the whist - ling Gyp - sy___ Rov - - er.
dy - ing day with my whist - ling Gyp - sy___ Rov - - er.

87

Ah dee doo, ah dee do da day. Ah da do, ah dee day dee. He

whist-led and he sang till the green woods rang, and he won the heart of a

la - - dy.

Long Time Ago
(High Voice)

American

1. On the lake where droop'd the wil-low long time a-go
2. Dwelt a maid be-loved and cher-ish'd by high and low

Where the rock threw back the bil-low bright-er than snow.
But with au-tumn leaf she per-ish'd long time a-go.

3. Rock   and tree and   flow - ing wa - ter   long   time a - go

4. While   to my fond   words she lis - ten'd   mur - mur - ing   low

Bird   and bee and   blos - som taught her   love's ___ spell to ___ know.

Ten - der - ly her   blue   eyes glis - ten'd   long ___ time a - go.

2nd time–Rit.

Long Time Ago
(Low Voice)

American

1. On the lake where droop'd the wil - low long time a - go
2. Dwelt a maid be - lov'd and cher - ish'd by high and — low

Where the rock threw back the bil - low bright - er than snow.
But with au - tumn leaf she per - ish'd long — time a - go.

3. Rock and tree and flow - ing wa - ter long time a - go
4. While to my fond words she lis - ten'd mur - mur - ing_ low

Bird and bee and blos - som taught her love's ___ spell to _ know.
Ten - der - ly her blue eyes glis - ten'd long ___ time a - go.

2nd time—Rit.

The Riddle Song

English

1. I

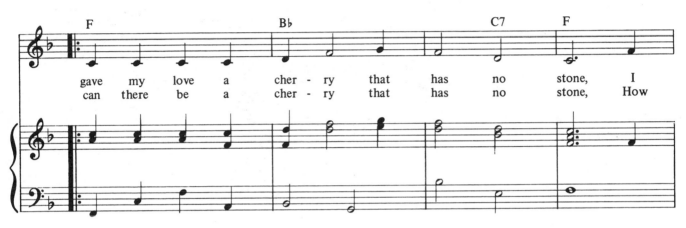

gave my love a cher - ry that has no stone, I
can there be a cher - ry that has has no stone, How

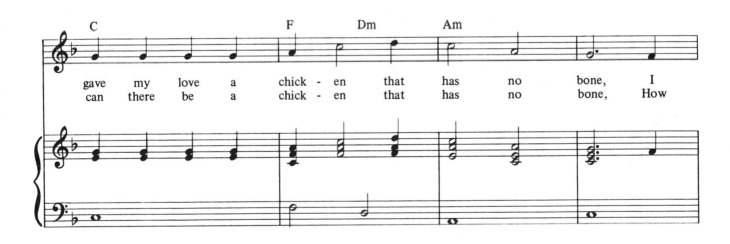

gave my love a chick - en that has no bone, I
can there be a chick - en that has no bone, How

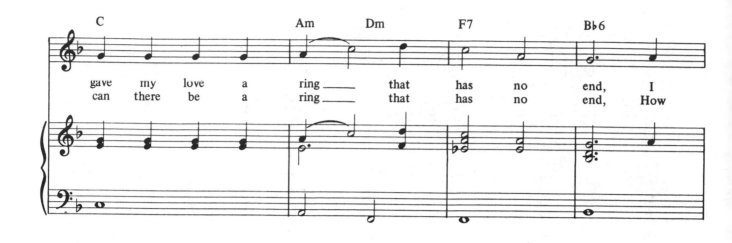

gave my love a ring ___ that has no end, I
can there be a ring ___ that has no end, How

gave my love a ba - by with no cry - in'. 2. How
can there be a ba - by with no cry -

1.

2.

in'?

94

3. A cher - ry when it's bloom - ing, it has no stone, A chick - en when it's pip - ping, it has no bone, A ring when it is roll - ing, it has no end, A ba - by when it's sleep - ing, there's no cry - in'.

Simple Gifts

American
Shaker Tune

love and de - light. When true sim - plic - i - ty is gain'd, to

bow and to bend we shan't be a - sham'd, To turn, turn will

be our de - light, Till by turn - ing, turn - ing we come 'round right.

97

Turn Ye to Me
(High Voice)

Scottish

The stars are shin - ing cheer - i - ly cheer - i - ly, ho - ro, mhai - ri dhu, turn ye___ to me, the sea - mew is moan - ing drear - i - ly, drear - i - ly, ho - ro, mhai - ri dhu, turn ye___ to me. Cold is the storm-wind that ruf - fles his breast, but

warm are the dow-ny plumes lin-ing his nest. Cold blows the storm there,

soft falls the snow there, ho - ro; mhai-ri-dhu; turn ye to me.

The waves are danc - ing

mer - ri - ly, mer - ri - ly, ho - ro, mhai-ri dhu, turn ye to me. The

Turn Ye to Me
(Low Voice)

Scottish

The stars are shin - ing cheer - i - ly, cheer - i - ly, ho - ro, mhai - ri dhu, turn ye to me, the sea-mew is moan - ing drear - i - ly, drear - i - ly, ho - ro, mhai - ri dhu, turn ye to me. Cold is the storm-wind that ruf - fles his breast, but

warm are the dow-ny plumes lin-ing his nest. Cold blows the storm there,

soft falls the snow there, ho - ro, mhai-ri dhu; turn ye to me.

The waves are danc-ing

mer-ri-ly, mer-ri-ly, ho - ro, mhai-ri dhu, turn ye to me. The

The Water Is Wide

British

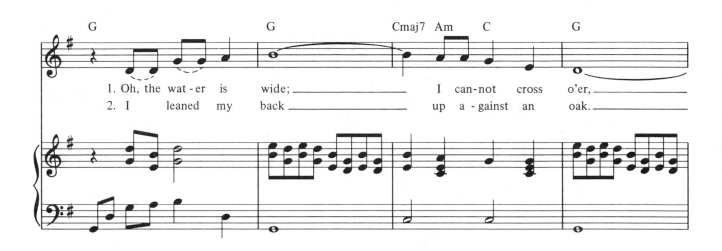

1. Oh, the wat-er is wide; _____ I can-not cross o'er, _____

2. I leaned my back _____ up a-gainst an oak. _____

_____ and nei-ther have I _____ wings _____ to _____ fly, _____

_____ I thought it was _____ a trust-y _____ tree, _____

104

but give me a boat that will car-ry two
but first it ben-ded and then it broke

and both shall row, my love and I.
as did my false, false lord to me.

Oh, love is sweet and love is fair,

105

When Love Is Kind

(High Voice)

Old melody

When love is

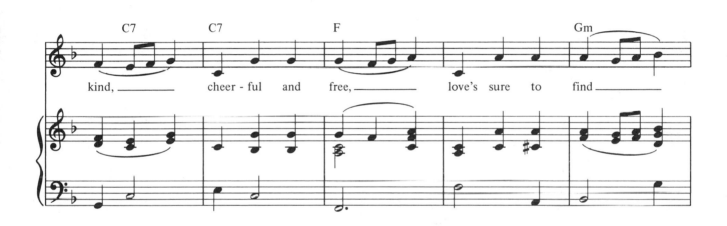

kind, _____ cheer - ful and free, _____ love's sure to find _____

wel - come from me; but when love brings _____ heart - ache and

pang, _____ tears and such things _____ love may go hang.

If love can sigh, _____ for one a - lone, _____ well pleased am I _____

to be that one; but should I see _____ love giv'n to rove, _____

to two, or three _____ then good - bye love.

Love must in short _____ keep fond and true, _____ through good re-
port, _____ and e-vil too; else here I swear, _____ young love may go, _____ for aught I care, _____ to Je-ri-
cho! Ah _____ Ha! Ha! Ha! to Je-ri-cho!

When Love Is Kind
(Low Voice)

Old melody

Gracefully

When love is

kind, _____ cheer - ful and free, _____ love's sure to find _____

wel - come from me; but when love brings _____ heart - ache and

pang, _____ tears and such things _____ love may go hang.

If love can sigh, _____ for one a - lone, _____ well pleased am I _____

to be that one; but should I see _____ love giv'n to rove, _____

to two, or three _____ then good - bye love.

Love must in short keep fond and true, through good re-port, and e-vil too; else here I swear, young love may go, for aught I care, to Je-ri-cho! Ah Ha! Ha! Ha! to Je-ri-cho!

Songs from Musical Theater

Almost Like Being
in Love

Words by
Alan Jay Lerner

Music by
Frederick Loewe

Lyrics: May-be the sun gave me the pow'r, but I could swim Loch Lom-ond and be home in half an hour. May-be the air gave me the drive for I'm all a-glow and a-live.

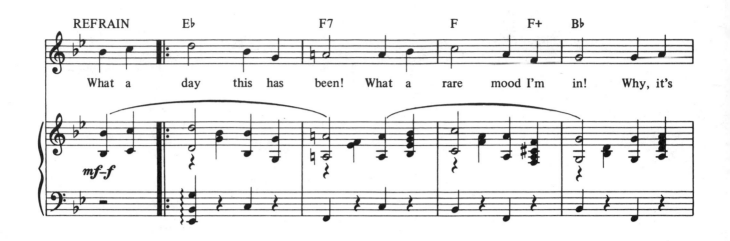

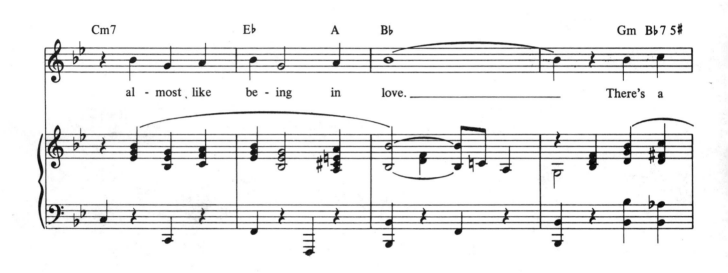

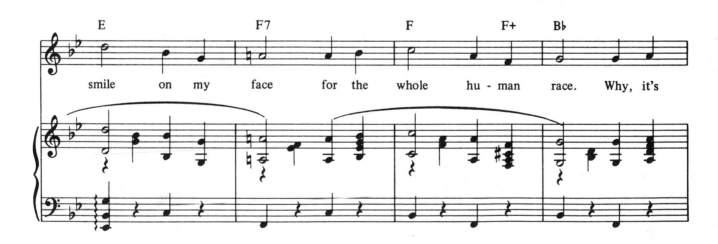

116

feel when that bell starts to peal I would swear I was

fall - ing, I could swear I was fall - ing, It's al - most like

be - ing in love._____ What a love._____

Climb Ev'ry Mountain
(High Voice)

Words by
Oscar Hammerstein II

Music by
Richard Rodgers

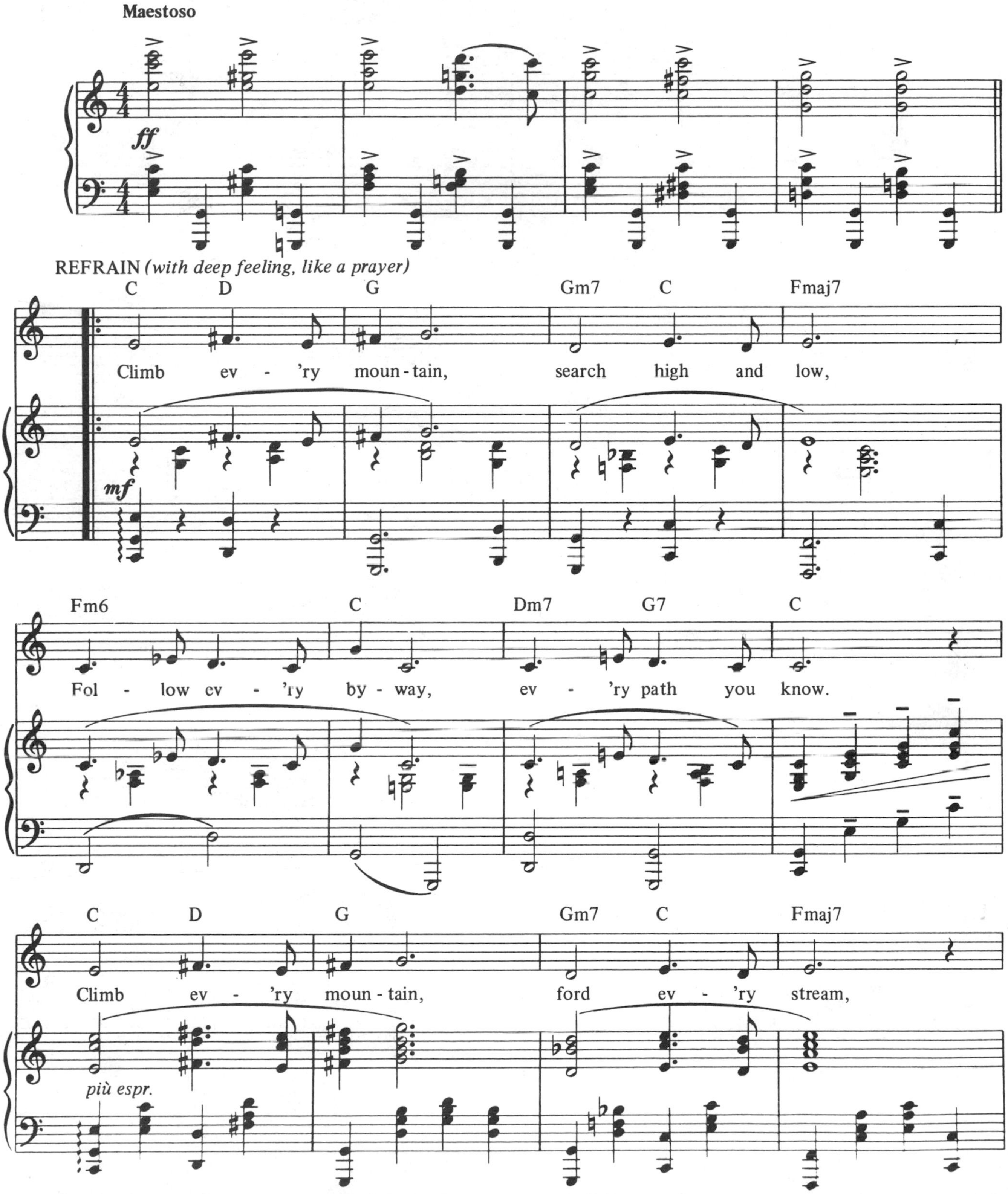

Maestoso
ff
REFRAIN (with deep feeling, like a prayer)
C D G Gm7 C Fmaj7
Climb ev - 'ry moun - tain, search high and low,
mf
Fm6 C Dm7 G7 C
Fol - low ev - 'ry by - way, ev - 'ry path you know.
C D G Gm7 C Fmaj7
Climb ev - 'ry moun - tain, ford ev - 'ry stream,
più espr.

Climb Ev'ry Mountain
(Low Voice)

Words by
Oscar Hammerstein II

Music by
Richard Rodgers

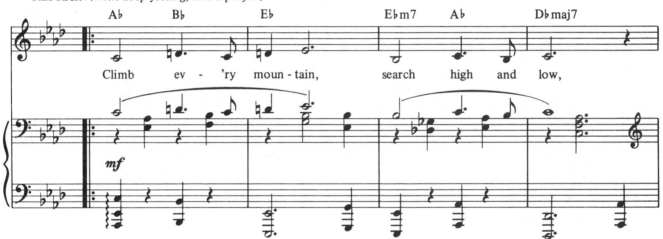

REFRAIN *(with deep feeling, like a prayer)*

Climb ev - 'ry moun - tain, search high and low,

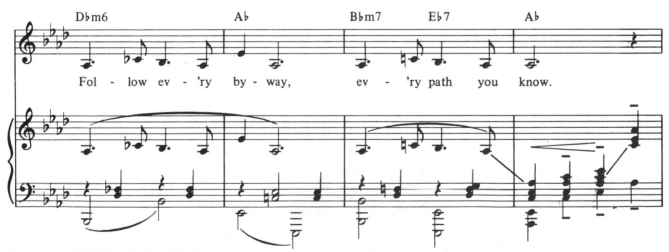

Fol - low ev - 'ry by - way, ev - 'ry path you know.

Allargando

Cm F Bb Bb7 Eb F7 Bb

for as long as you live. _____ Climb ev - 'ry moun-tain,

molto cresc.

f *legato*

Bbm7 Eb Abmaj7 Fm Fm7 Bbm Bbm7 Ab Ab+ Ab7+

ford ev - 'ry stream, Fol - low ev - 'ry rain-bow till you

piu cresc. e poco a poco allarg.

ff

Db6 Eb7 **1.** Ab Db Eb **2.** Ab Bbm7 Ab

find your dream! dream!

ff *marcato*

In a Simple Way
I Love You

Words by
Gretchen Cryer

Music by
Nancy Ford

I'm here to see you through. I'll make mu - sic while you

sing your song while you do what you have to do.

I'll be be - side you rain or shine,— Love has man - y fac - es, and

one of them___ is___ mine.

Look Over There
(High Voice)

Music and lyrics by
Jerry Herman

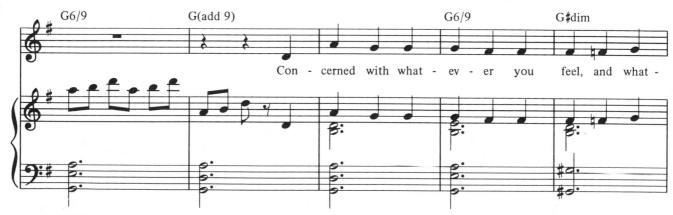

When your world spins too fast and your bub-ble has burst, some-one puts him-self last so that you can come first.

Look Over There
(Low Voice)

Music and lyrics by
Jerry Herman

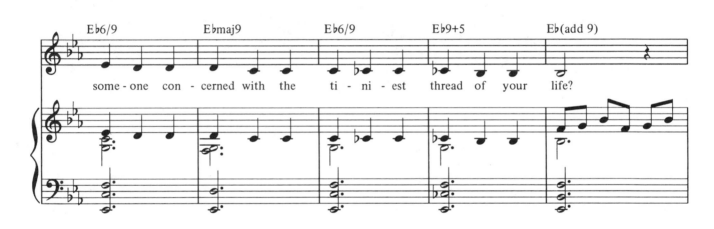

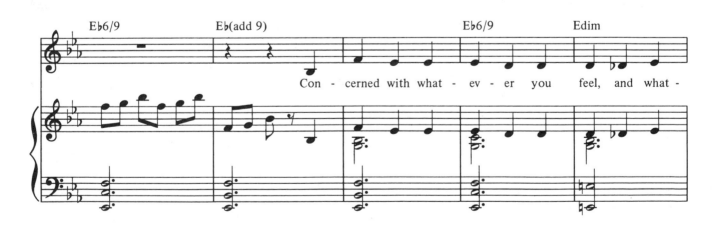

need them with - out be - ing told? When you have a

hurt in your heart your too proud to dis - close?

Look o - ver there, Look o - ver there;

Some - bod - y al - ways

So count all the loves who will love you from now 'til the end of your life. And when you have add - ed the loves who have loved you be - fore, Look o - ver there;

Make Someone Happy

Words by
Betty Comend
and Aldolph Green

Music by
Jule Styne

140

142

Not a Day Goes By

Stephen Sondheim

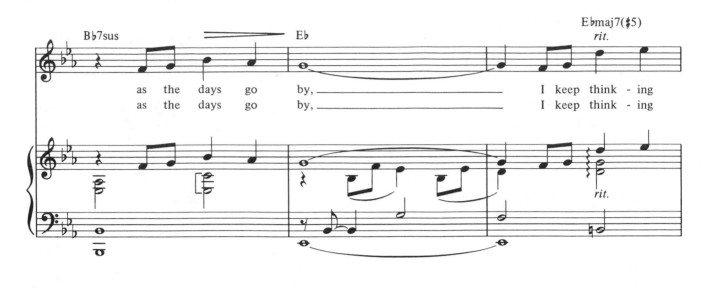

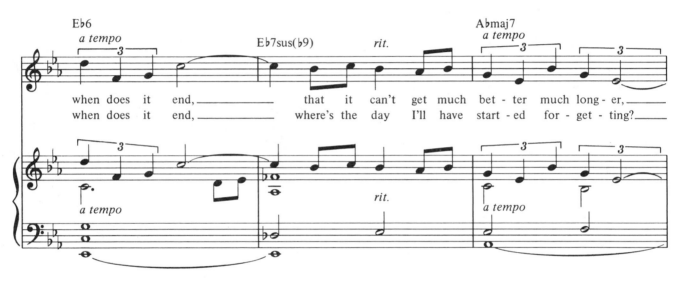

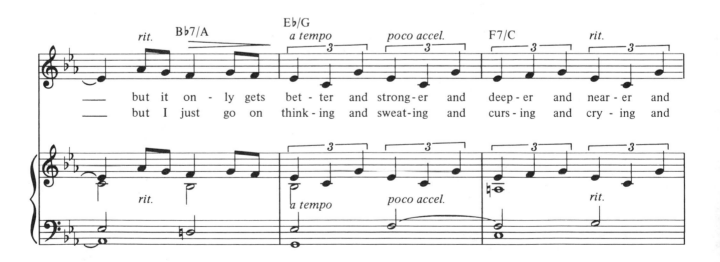

144

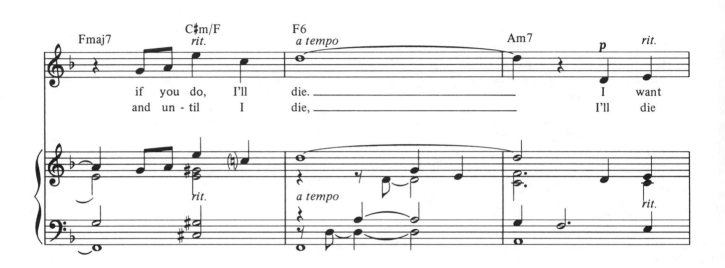

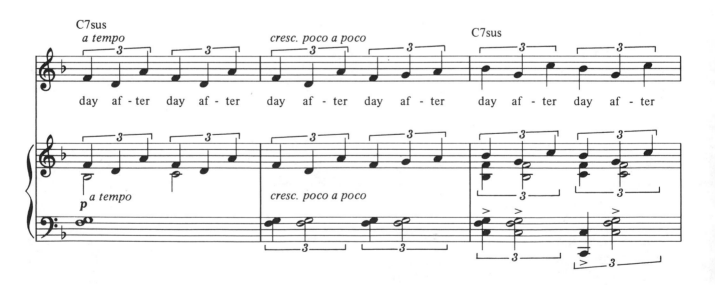

On a Clear Day
(You Can See Forever)

Words by
Alan Jay Lerner

Music by
Burton Lane

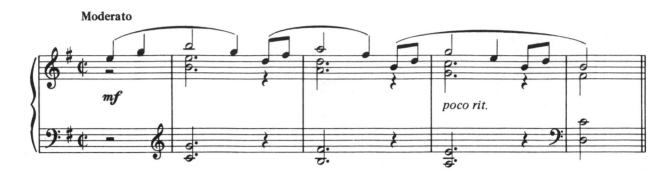

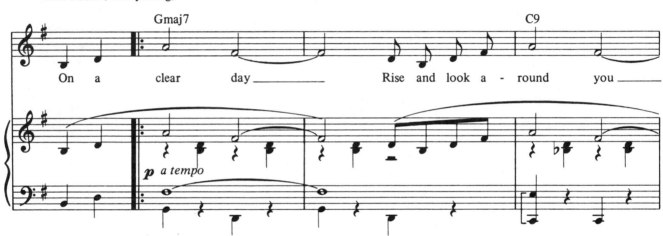

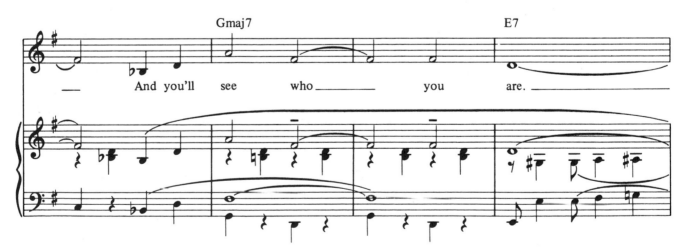

On a clear day _____ How it will as - tound you _____

That the glow of your be - ing out - shines ev - 'ry

star. You feel part of _____ ev - 'ry moun - tain, sea and shore. _____

149

You can hear, from far and near, a world you've nev - er heard be - fore.

And on a clear day, On that clear day

You can see for - ev - er and ev -

People

Words by
Bob Merrill

Music by
Jule Styne

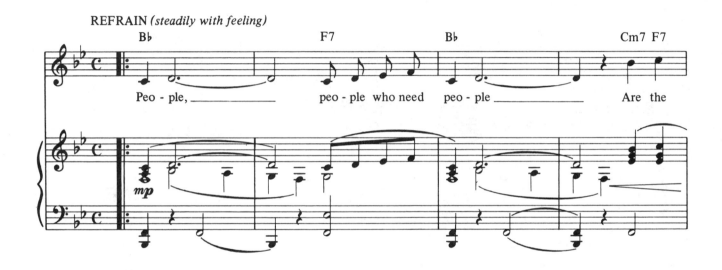

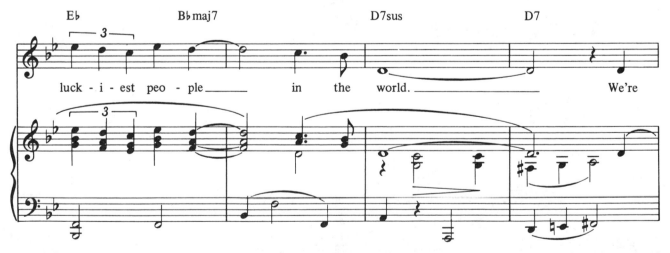

155

Put On a Happy Face

Words by
Lee Adams

Lyrics and
Music by
Lee Adams, Charles Strouse

Wipe off that "full of doubt" look, ___ Slap on a hap-py grin! And spread sun-shine all o-ver the place, Just Put On A

Hap-py Face!

Face! ___

Send in the Clowns

Music and Lyrics
Stephen Sondheim

bliss?   Don't you ap - prove?   One who keeps

tear - ing a - round,   one who can't   move. . .   Where are the

clowns?   Send in the clowns.   Just when I'd

stopped o - pen - ing doors. Fin - al - ly

know-ing the one that I want-ed was yours, mak-ing my

en - trance a - gain with my u - su - al flair, sure of my

lines,   no one is there.

Don't you love farce?   My fault I
rich?   Is - n't it

fear.   I thought that you'd want what I want, sor - ry my
queer?   Los - ing my tim - ing this late in my car -

dear.
reer? But where are the clowns?
And where are the clowns? Quick, send in the
There ought to be

1.

clowns. Don't both-er they're here. Is-n't it

2.

clowns. Well, may - be next year. . .

ten.

rit.

163

Summertime
(High Voice)

Words by
DuBose Heyward

Music by
George Gershwin

Summertime
(Low Voice)

Lyric by
DuBose Heyward

Music by
George Gershwin

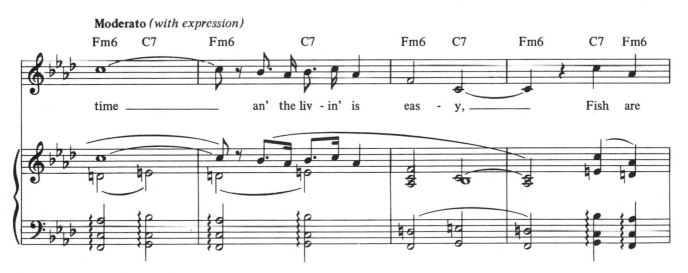

167

jump - in', _____ an' the cot - ton is high. _____

Oh yo' dad - dy's rich, _____ an' yo' ma is good - look - in', _____ So hush, lit - tle ba - by,

The Sweetest Sounds

Words and
Music by
Richard Rodgers

Tomorrow Belongs to Me

Lyrics by
Fred Ebb

Music by
John Kander

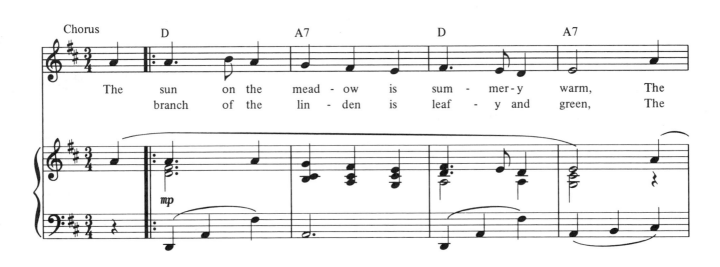

The sun on the mead-ow is sum-mer-y warm, The
branch of the lin-den is leaf-y and green, The

stag in the for-est runs free; _____ The
rage has de-sert-ed the sea; _____ The

heart   as   a   shel - ter   de - fies   the   storm,
world   holds   a   prom - ise   that   shines   un - seen,   TO - MOR - ROW BE -

LONGS   TO   ME. _____   The

ME. _____   The

175

What I Did for Love
(High Voice)

Words by
Edward Kleban

Music by
Marvin Hamlisch

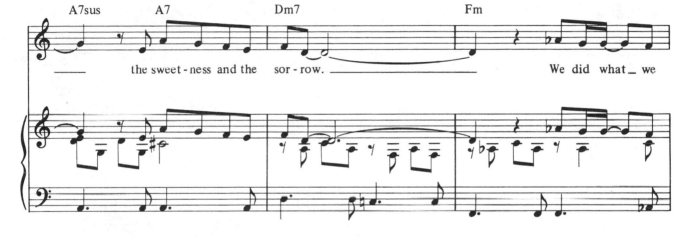

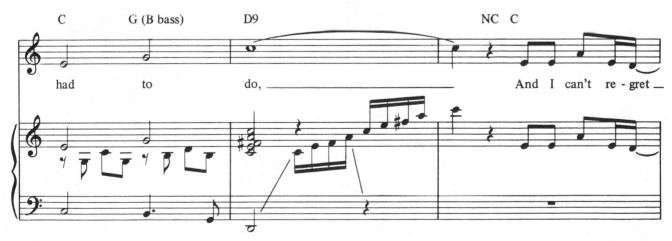

WHAT I DID FOR LOVE from "A Chorus Line." © 1975 MARVIN HAMLISCH, INC. and EDWARD KLEBAN.
All Rights Controlled By WREN MUSIC CO. and AMERICAN COMPASS MUSIC CORP. International
Copyright Secured. All Rights Reserved. Used by Permission.

What I Did for Love
(Low Voice)

Words by
Edward Kleban

Music by
Marvin Hamlisch

Kiss to-day_ good - bye, _____

_____ the sweet - ness and the sor - row. _____ We did what_ we

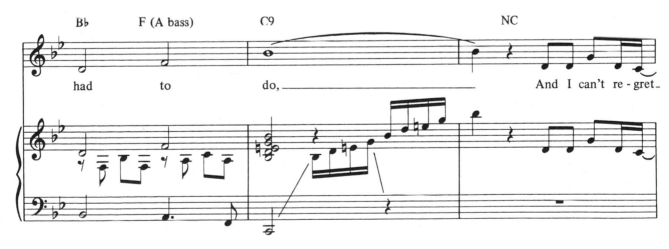

had to do, _____ And I can't re - gret_

184

Who Can I Turn To
(When Nobody Needs Me)

Words and
music by
Leslie Bricusse
and
Anthony Newley

Who can I turn to_____ when no-bod-y needs me?_____ My
heart wants to know and so I must go where des-ti-ny leads me._____ With

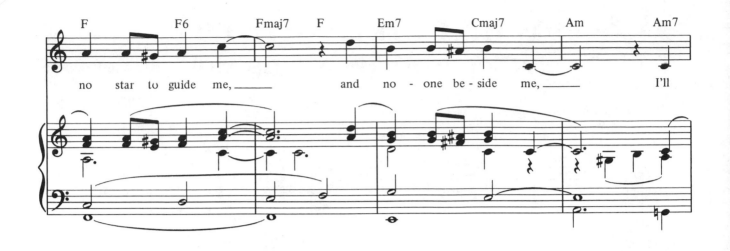

no star to guide me,_____ and no - one be - side me,_____ I'll

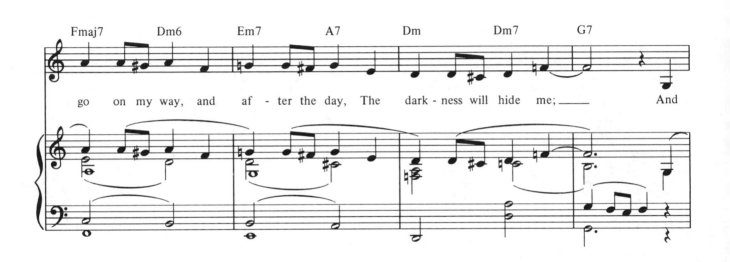

go on my way, and af - ter the day, The dark - ness will hide me;_____ And

may - be to - mor - row_____ I'll find what I'm af - ter_____ I'll

Art Songs and Arias

An den Mond
To the Moon
(High Voice)

Words by
Goethe

Music by
Franz Schubert

1. Fullest wieder Busch und Thal
     still mit Nebel glanz,
   lösest endlich auch einmal meine
     Seele ganz;
   breitest über mein Gefild lindernd
     deinen Blick,
   wie des Freundes Ange mild über
     mein Geschick.

2. Jeden Nachklang fühlt mein Herz
     froh und trüber Zeit,
   wandle zwischen Freud, und
     Schmerz in der Einsamkeit.

   Fliesse, fliesse lieber Fluss!
     Nimmer werd' ich froh;
   so verrauschte Scherz und Kuss,
     und die Treue so.

3. Selig, wer sich vor der Welt ohne
     Hass verschliesst,
   einen Freund am Busen hält und
     mit dem geniesst,
   was von Menschen nicht gewusst,
     oder nicht bedacht,
   durch das Labyrinth der Brust
     wandelt in der Nacht.

1. You fill the bush and valley
     quietly with misty shine,
   You relax, for once and for all, my
     soul totally;
   You spread over my domain your
     softening glance,
   like a friend's eye mildly over my
     fate.

2. Every echo my heart feels of joy or
     sadness,
   I walk between joy and sadness in
     loneliness, happiness and
     depression.
   Flow, flow beloved stream! Never
     will I be happy;
   since playing and kissing die
     away, and fidelity likewise.

3. Blessed he who closes himself off
     from the world without hate,
   One friend he holds to his bosom,
     and with that one,
   enjoys what men do not know,
     or have not considered,
   through the labyrinth of the heart,
     he wanders through the night.

Ziemlich langsam

1. Füll - est wie - der Busch und Thal still mit Ne - bel - glanz,
2. Je - den Nach - klang fühlt mein Herz froh und trü - ber Zeit,
3. Se - lig, wer sich vor der Welt oh - ne Hass ver - schliesst,

lös - est end - lich auch ein - mal mei - ne See - le___ ganz;_____
wan - dle zwi - schen Freud' und___Schmerz in der Ein - sam - keit._____
ei - nen Freund am Bu - sen___hält und mit dem ge - niesst,_____

breit - est ü - ber mein___ Ge - fild' lin - dernd dei - nen Blick,_____
Flie - sse, flie - sse, lie - ber Fluss! Nim - mer werd' ich froh;_____
was von Men - schen nicht___ ge - wusst, o - der nicht be - dacht,_____

wie des___Freun - des Au - ge mild ü - ber___mein___Ge - schick._____
so___ ver - rausch - te Scherz___und Kuss, und___die Treu - e so._____
durch___das La - by - rinth___der Brust wan - delt___in der___Nacht._____

Words by
Goethe

Music by
Franz Schubert

An den Mond
To the Moon
(Low Voice)

1. Füllest wieder Busch und Thal
   still mit Nebel glanz,
   lösest endlich auch einmal meine
   Seele ganz;
   breitest über mein Gefild lindernd
   deinen Blick,
   wie des Freundes Ange mild über
   mein Geschick.

2. Jeden Nachklang fühlt mein Herz
   froh und trüber Zeit,
   wandle zwischen Freud, und
   Schmerz in der Einsamkeit.

   Fliesse, fliesse lieber Fluss!
   Nimmer werd' ich froh;
   so verrauschte Scherz und Kuss,
   und die Treue so.

3. Selig, wer sich vor der Welt ohne
   Hass verschliesst,
   einen Freund am Busen hält und
   mit dem geniesst,
   was von Menschen nicht gewusst,
   oder nicht bedacht,
   durch das Labyrinth der Brust
   wandelt in der Nacht.

1. You fill the bush and valley
   quietly with misty shine,
   You relax, for once and for all, my
   soul totally;
   You spread over my domain your
   softening glance,
   like a friend's eye mildly over my
   fate.

2. Every echo my heart feels of joy or
   sadness,
   I walk between joy and sadness in
   loneliness, happiness and
   depression.
   Flow, flow beloved stream! Never
   will I be happy;
   since playing and kissing die
   away, and fidelity likewise.

3. Blessed he who closes himself off
   from the world without hate,
   One friend he holds to his bosom,
   and with that one,
   enjoys what men do not know,
   or have not considered,
   through the labyrinth of the heart,
   he wanders through the night.

Ziemlich langsam

1. Füll - est wie - der Busch und Thal still mit Ne - bel - glanz,
2. Je - den Nach - klang fühlt mein Herz froh und trü - ber Zeit,
3. Se - lig, wer sich vor der Welt oh - ne Hass ver - schliesst,

lös-est end-lich auch __ ein-mal   mei - ne See - le __ ganz; _____
wan-dle zwis-chen Freud' __ und __ Schmerz   in   der Ein-sam - keit. _____
ei - nen Freund am Bu-sen __ hält   und mit dem __ ge - niesst, _____

breit-est ü - ber mein __ Ge-fild'   lin-dernd dei-nen Blick, _____
Flie-sse, flie-sse, lie - ber Fluss! Nim-mer werd' ich froh; _____
was von Men-schen nicht __ ge-wusst, o - der nicht be - dacht, _____

wie __ des __ Freun - des Au-ge __ mild   ü - ber __ mein __ Ge - schick. _____
so __ ver - rausch - te Scherz __ und __ Kuss, und die Treu-e __ so. _____
durch __ das __ La - by - rinth __ der __ Brust wan-delt __ in __ der __ Nacht. _____

Beneath a Weeping Willow's Shade

Piano arr. adapted
from the original by
Roy S. Stoughton

Words and
Music by
Francis Hopkinson
(1737–1791)

heart she laid, And plain - tive was her moan, And plain - tive was her moan.
dieu," she cried, "I ne'er shall see thee more, I ne'er shall see thee more."

The mock - bird sat up - on a bough, The

mock - bird sat up - on a bough And lis - ten'd to her lay, Then

to the dis - tant hills he bore The dul - cet notes a - way, Then

to the dis - tant hills he bore The dul - cet notes a - way, The

dul - cet notes a - way, The dul - cet notes a - way. way.

197

Cara e dolce

Alessandro Scarlatti
(1659–1725)

Cara e dolce, dolcissima libertá,
quanto ti piange il core,
fra i lacci d'un crin d'oro prova d'un
ciglio arcier la credelta.
le dure ritorte, che rigida sorte mi dá
per mercé mi stringono il pié e al
mio lungo penar negan pietà.

Dear and sweet, sweetest liberty,
How much the heart weeps for you!
In the snares of golden hair the
eyebrow archer uses cruelty.
The hard fetters that rigid fate gave
me bind my feet and deny pity
from lasting pain.

Used with kind permission of Edition Wilhelm Hansen A/S Copenhagen. Edited by Kend Jeppeson.

cor-re fra i lac-ci d'un crin d'o-ro pro-va d'un cig-lio ar-cier la cru - del -

tà. Ca - ra e dol - ce dol - ce, ca - ra e dol - ce dol - ce, dol -

cis - si-ma li - ber - tà, dol - cis - si - ma, dol-cis-si-ma li - ber - tà,

le du-re ri - tor - te, che ri - gi-da sor - te mi dà per mer -

cè mi strin - go - no il piè, mi strin - go - no il piè e al mio lun - go pe - nar ne - gan pie -

tà, ne - gan pie - tà, e al mio lun - go pe - nar ne - gan pie -

tà. Ca - ra e dol - ce dol - ce, dol - cis - si - ma li - ber -

tà, dol - cis - si - ma, dol - cis - si - ma li - ber-tà, dol - cis - si - ma li - ber-tà.

Come Again, Sweet Love

John Dowland
(1562–1626)
Piano arr. by
Roy S. Stoughton

a tempo
p *poco a poco cresc.*

To see,   to hear,   to touch,   to kiss,
I sit,   I sigh,   I weep,   I faint,
Her eyes   of fire,   her heart   of flint

p *a tempo*   *poco a poco cresc.*

mf   *mp*

to die, _____   With thee a -
I die, _____   In dead - ly
is made, _____   Whom tears nor

mf   *mp*

rit. e dim.   *p*

gain   in   sweet - est   sym   pa - thy.
pain   and   end - less   mis   er - y.
truth   may   once   in   vade.

rit. e dim.   *p*

The Daisies
(High Voice)

Samuel Barber,
Op. 2, No. 1
(1910–)

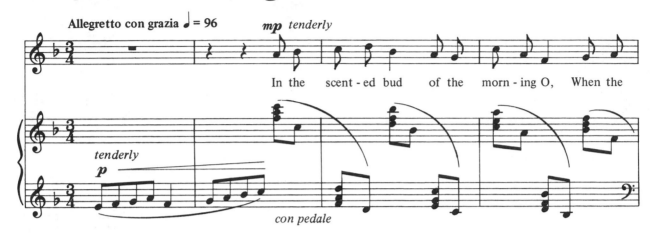

wan-dered hap-p'ly, to and fro, I kissed my dear on ei-ther cheek, In the

bud of the morn-ing O! A lark sang up, from the

breez-y land; A lark sang down, from a cloud a-far; As she and

I went, hand in hand, In the field where the dais-ies are.

The Daisies
(Low Voice)

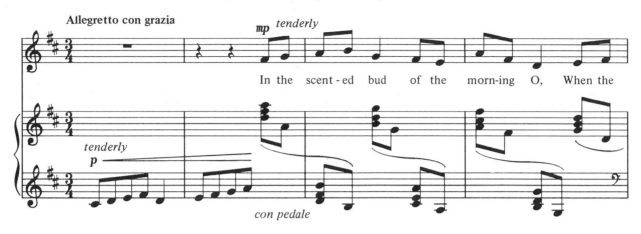

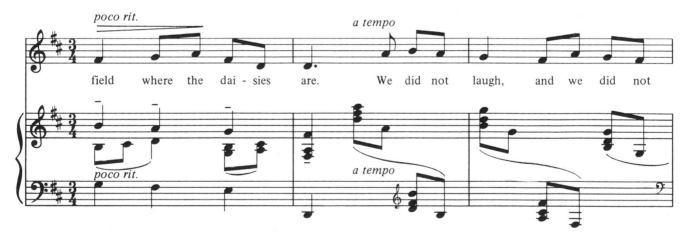

Dolce scherza

G. A. Perti
(1661–1756)

Dolce scherza e dolce ride	Sweetly play and sweetly laugh
Vago labbro e spira amor;	Lips, which inspire my love;
Ma t'alletta e poi t'uccide,	But they entice you and then destroy you,
Cosi affligge questo cor.	Thus afflicting my heart.

Andantino

Dol - ce_____ scher - za_ e dol - ce_____ ri - de

Va - go_____ lab - bro_ e spi - ra a - mor; Ma t'al -

let - ta_ e poi t'uc - ci - de Co - si_ af -

flig - ge___ que - sto cor. Dol - ce___

scher - za___ e dol - ce___ ri - de va - go___

lab - bro___ e spi - ra a - mor, dol - ce___

ri - de e spi - ra a - mor.___

colla voce

dolcissimo

calando

E'en As a Lovely Flower
(High Voice)

Kate Kroeker,
after Heine

Frank Bridge

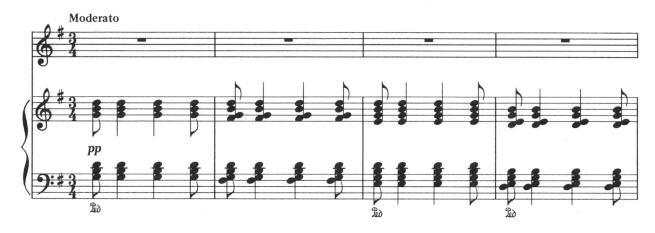

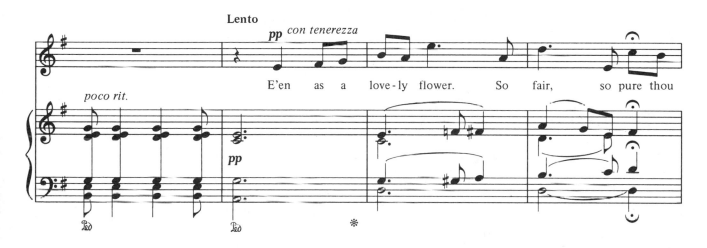

pure, _____ and fair.

E'en as a love-ly flower, so fair, so pure thou art. _____

E'en As a Lovely Flower

(Low Voice)

Kate Kroeker,
after Heine

Frank Bridge

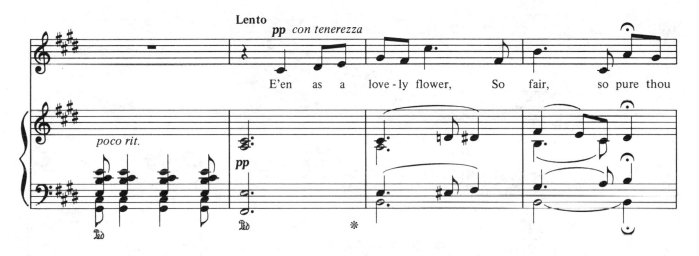

E'en as a love-ly flower, So fair, so pure thou art,

art, I gaze on

214

pure, _____ and fair. _____

E'en as a love-ly flower, so fair, so pure thou

art. _____

English version
by Dr. Theodore
Baker

Lasciatemi morire!
No longer let me languish
Canto from the opera *Ariana*
(High Voice)

Claudio
Monteverdi
(1587–1643)

Lasciatemi morire!
E che volete che mi conforte
in cosi durasorte,
in cosi gran martire?
Lasciatemi morire!

Let me die!
And what can you do to comfort me
In this difficult situation,
In this great martyrdom?
Let me die!

in co - sì du - ra sor - te, in co - sì gran mar -

ti - re? La - scia - te - mi mo - ri - re,

la - scia - te - mi mo - ri - re!

218

English version
by Dr. Theodore
Baker

Lasciatemi morire!
No longer let me languish
Canto from the opera *Ariana*
(Low Voice)

Claudio
Monteverdi
(1587–1643)

Lasciatemi morire!
E che volete che mi conforte
in cosi durasorte,
in cosi gran martire?
Lasciatemi morire!

Let me die!
And what can you do to comfort me
In this difficult situation,
In this great martyrdom?
Let me die!

Lullaby
(High Voice)

Words by
Christina Rossetti

Music by
Cyril Scott
Op. 57 No. 2

221

sleep - - ing, Lul - la -
by, Lul - la - by,
While the birds are si - lence keep -
ing, Lul - la - by, Oh

Lul - - la - by, _____ Sleep my

ba - by, fall a - sleep - - - ing _____

rit. *dim.*

rit.

Lul - - la - by, Oh,

p *rit.*

rit.

p

a tempo

Lul - - la - by, Lul - la -

a tempo

Lullaby
(Low Voice)

Words by
Christina Rossetti

Music by
Cyril Scott
Op. 57 No. 2

Lul - la - by, oh Lul - la -

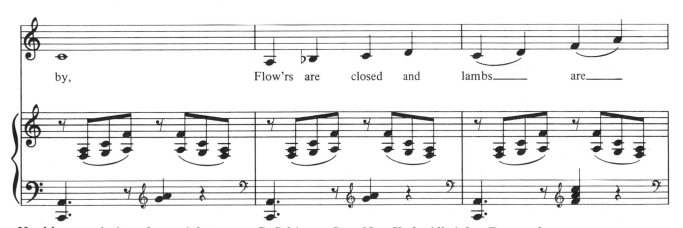

by, Flow'rs are closed and lambs___ are___

227

228

Nel cor più non mi sento

mi sento

Giovanni Paisiello
(1740–1816)

Why feels my heart
so dormant
Arietta
(High Voice)

Nel cor più non mi sento	The heart no more I feel
brillar la gioventu;	sparkle the youth;
cagion del mio tormento,	cause of my torment,
amor, se colpa tu.	love, you are the guilty one.
Mi pizzichi, mi stuzzichi,	You pinch me, you excite me,
mi pungichi, mi mastichi;	You sting me, you bite me;
che cosa è questo, ahime?	What thing is this anyway?
Pietà, pietà, pietà!	Have pity!
Amóre è un certo che	Love is a certain thing
che disperar mi fa!	which gives me despair!

Andantino ♩.= 58

dolce

cresc.

p

Nel cor più non mi sen - to bril - lar la___ gio - ven -

f

p

tù; ca - gion del mio tor - men - to, a -

mor, sei col - pa tu. Mi piz - zi - chi, mi stuz - zi - chi, mi

pun - gi - chi, mi mas - ti - chi; che co - sa è que - sto ahi - mè? pie -

tà, pie - tà, pie - tà! a - mo - re è un cer - to che, che

sf

p

di - spe-rar ___ mi fa.

Nel cor più non mi sento

Why feels my heart so dormant
Arietta
(Low Voice)

Giovanni Paisiello
(1740–1816)

Nel cor più non mi sento	The heart no more I feel
brillar la gioventu;	sparkle the youth;
cagion del mio tormento,	cause of my torment,
amor, se colpa tu.	love, you are the guilty one.
Mi pizzichi, mi stuzzichi,	You pinch me, you excite me,
mi pungichi, mi mastichi;	You sting me, you bite me;
che cosa è questo, ahime?	What thing is this anyway?
Pietà, pietà, pietà!	Have pity!
Amóre è un certo che	Love is a certain thing
che disperar mi fa!	which gives me despair!

Nel cor più non mi sen-to bril-lar la___ gio-ven-

tù;   ca - gion del mio___ tor - men - to, a -

mor, sei col - pa tu.   Mi piz - zi - chi, mi stuz - zi - chi,   mi

pun - gi - chi, mi mas-ti - chi;   che co - sa è que - sto ahi - mè?___ pie -

tà,___ pie - tà,___ pie - tà!   a - mo - re è un cer - to che,_____ che

di - spe - rar___ mi fa.

Now Is the Month of Maying

Music by
Thomas Morley
(1537–1602)
Piano arr. by
Roy S. Stoughton

1. Now is the month of May - ing, When mer - ry lads are play - ing.
2. The spring, clad all in glad - ness, Doth laugh at win - ter's sad - ness.
3. Fie, then, why sit we mus - ing, Sweet youth's de - light re - fus - ing?

Tra la la la la la la la la la la, La la la la la la la.

Each with his bon - ny lass
And to the bag - pipe's sound,
Say, dain - ty nymphs, and speak,

A -
The
Shall

dan - cing on the grass,
nymphs tread out their ground,
we play bar - ley break?

La la la la la,

La la la la la la la, la, la la la la.

O Lord on High

Words by
Virginia P. Marwick

Music by
W. A. Mozart
(1756–1791)

Lord on high, we pray Thee guide us, And keep our

souls in ___ Thine own care; When dark our way, with ___

light pro - vide us, Teach us Thy right - eous - ness to

share, — teach us Thy right - eous - ness to share.

Lead Thou us

on thro'— dan - gers low'r - ing, Be Thou our

shield in fears o'er - pow'r - ing; Oh, let Thy mer - cy e'er be our guard, — O - ver our life keep — watch and ward, — o - ver our life — keep watch and ward.

Sing a new song
Psalms 98 and 96
(High Voice)

Antonin Dvořák
(1841–1904)

Sing a new song un-to the Lord __ with glad - ness,

For with His right hand wrought He vic-to-ry.

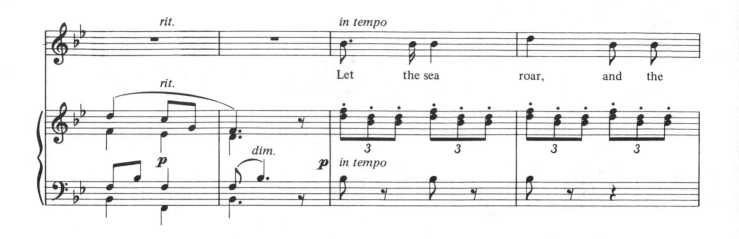

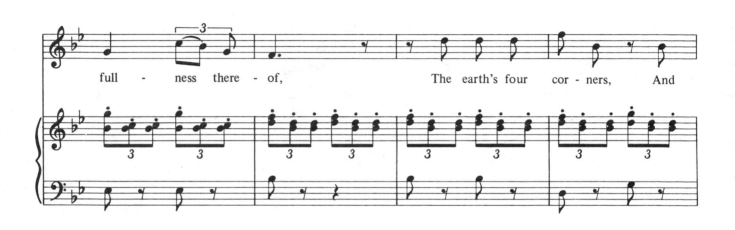

Let the floods clap their hands, Let all the hills be

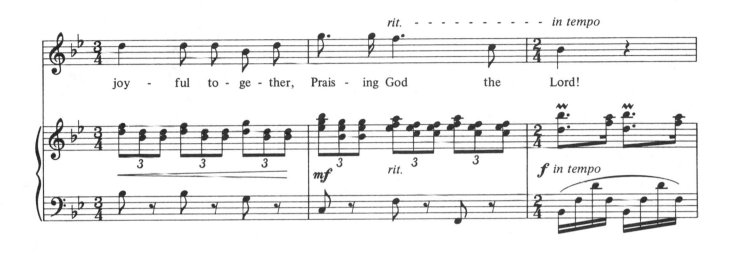

joy - ful to - ge - ther, Prais - ing God the Lord!

Fields and mea-dows re - joice to - ge-ther, Woods and_ for - ests_ be ye joy - ful be - fore the Lord.

Sing a new song
Psalms 98 and 96
(Low Voice)

Antonin Dvořák
(1841–1904)

Sing a new song un-to the Lord ___ with glad - ness,

For with His right hand wrought He vic - to-ry.

mezza voce

Let the heav'ns re - joice be-fore Him,

And let the earth be ___ glad!

in tempo

Let the sea roar, and the full - ness there - of, The earth's four cor - ners, And all with - in it dwell - ing!

Let the floods clap their hands, Let all the hills be

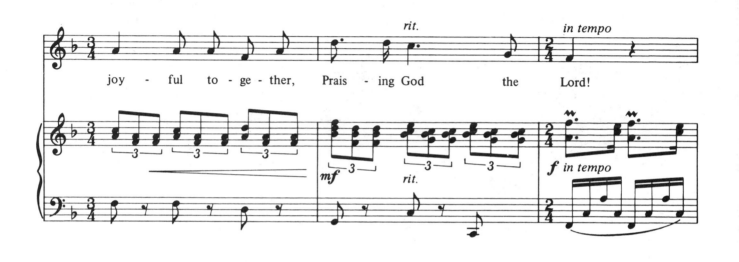

joy - ful to - ge - ther, Prais - ing God the Lord!

Fields and mea-dows re-joice to-ge-ther, Woods and for-ests be ye joy-ful be-fore the Lord.

con Ped.

Where'er you walk

G. F. Handel
(1685–1759)

From *Semele*
(High Voice)

Largo e pianissimo per tutto

Wher - e'er you walk, cool gales shall fan the glades; Trees, where you sit, shall crowd in - to a shade, Trees where you sit shall crowd in -

to _____ a shade;

Wher - e'er you walk, cool gales shall fan the glade;

Trees, where you sit, shall crowd in - to a_ shade. _____

Trees, where you sit,

shall crowd _____ in - to _____ a shade.

Fine

Wher - e'er you tread, the blush - ing flow'rs shall rise, and all things flour - ish, And all things flour - ish, wher - e'er you turn your eyes, wher - e'er you turn your eyes, wher-e'er you turn your eyes.

Adagio

D. C.

253

Where'er you walk

From *Semele*
(Low Voice)

G. F. Handel
(1685–1759)

Largo e pianissimo per tutto

Wher - e'er you walk, cool gales shall fan the glade; Trees, where you_ sit, shall crowd in - to a shade, Trees where you_ sit shall crowd in -

to _____ a shade;

(un poco più f)

Wher - e'er you walk, cool gales shall fan the glade;

(pp)

Trees where you sit, shall crowd in - to a ___ shade, _____

Trees, where you sit, shall crowd in - to a shade.

f

Fine

Wher - e'er you tread, the blush - ing flow'rs shall rise, and all things flour - ish, And all things flour - ish, wher - e'er you turn your eyes, wher - e'er you turn your eyes, wher-e'er you turn your eyes.

Adagio

D. C.

Widmung
(High Voice)

Wolfgang Müller
(1816–1873)
Translated by
Arthur Westbrook

Robert Franz,
Op. 14, No. 1
(1815–1892)

O danke nicht für diese Lieder,
mir ziemt es dankbar Dir zu sein;
Du gabst sie mir,
ich gebe wieder,
was jetzt und einst und ewig Dein.
Dein sind sie alle gewesen.
Aus Deiner lieben Augen Licht
hab ich sie treulich abgelesen,
kennst Du die eignen Lieder nicht?

Oh do not thank me for these songs,
I should be thankful to you;
You gave them to me,
I give back again,
what was and always will be yours.
They have all been yours.
In the light of your dear eyes
I have read them faithfully,
Don't you recognize your own songs?

258

e - wig Dein. Dein sind sie

al - le ja ge - we - sen. Aus Dei - ner

lie - ben Au - gen Licht hab' ich sie treu - lich

Wolfgang Müller
(1816–1873)
Translated by
Arthur Westbrook

Widmung
(Low Voice)

Robert Franz,
Op. 14, No. 1
(1815–1892)

O danke nicht für diese Lieder,
mir ziemt es dankbar Dir zu sein;
Du gabst sie mir,
ich gebe wieder,
was jetzt und einst und ewig Dein.
Dein sind sie alle gewesen.
Aus Deiner lieben Augen Licht
hab ich sie treulich abgelesen,
kennst Du die eignen Lieder nicht?

Oh do not thank me for these songs,
I should be thankful to you;
You gave them to me,
I give back again,
what was and always will be yours.
They have all been yours.
In the light of your dear eyes
I have read them faithfully,
Don't you recognize your own songs?

lie - ben Au - gen Licht   hab' ich sie treu - lich

ab - ge - le - sen,   kennst Du die

eig - nen Lie - der nicht? _____

263

kennst Du die eig - nen Lie - der nicht?

Rounds

A round is a composition in which all voices sing the same music, but begin at different and specified times. To be most effective musically, the same care should be afforded dynamics and phrasing that is typically given to the study of other styles of music. Beginning with a unison effort, rounds can be a useful and entertaining way to develop basic skills in part singing.

Alleluia

Unknown

(2 part)

1. Al - le - lu - ia, Al - le - lu - ia, A - men, A - men.

Come, Follow, Follow

John Hilton
(1599–1657)

(3 parts)

1. Come, fol - low, fol - low, fol - low, fol - low, fol - low, fol - low me.

2. Whith - er shall I fol - low, fol - low, fol - low, whith - er shall I fol - low, fol - low thee?

3. To the green - wood, to the green - wood, to the green - wood, green - wood tree.

Die Musici—Music Alone Shall Live

German Canon

(3 parts)

1. All things shall per - ish from un - der the sky;
Him - mel und Er - de müs - sen ver - gehn;

2. Mu - sic a - lone shall live; Mu - sic a - lone shall live;
A - ber die Mus - i - ci; A - ber die Mus - i - ci;

3. Mu - sic a - lone shall live ne - ver to die.
A - ber die Mus - i - ci blei - ben be - stehn.

Haste Thee Nymph

F. Arnold

(3 part)

Allegretto

1. Haste thee nymph, and bring with thee jest and youth - ful jol - li - ty,

2. Quips, and cranks, and wan - ton wiles, Nods, and becks, and wreath - ed smiles,

3. Sport that wrin - kled care de - rides, And laugh - ter hold - ing both his sides.

268

Let Us Sing Together

(4 part)

1. Let us sing to - geth - er, Let us sing to - geth - er, One and all a joy - ous song.

2. Let us sing to - geth - er, One and all a joy - ous song.

3. Let us sing a - gain and a - gain, Let us sing a - gain and a - gain,

Make New Friends

(4 parts)

Moderately Slow

Make new friends but keep the old; one is sil - ver and the oth - er gold.

O Give Thanks

(2 parts)

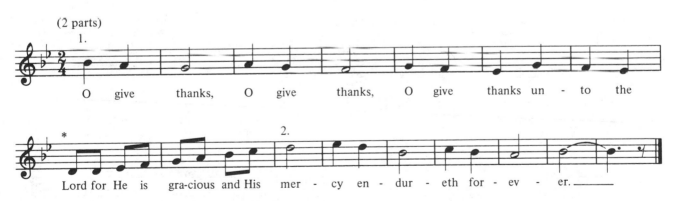

O give thanks, O give thanks, O give thanks un - to the

Lord for He is gra - cious and His mer - cy en - dur - eth for - ev - er.

* When sung as a grace, group 1 sings through once and from the beginning to * again, while group 2 (coming in at 2) sings through once.

Rise Up, O Flame

Christoph Pragiorius

Rise up, O flame, _____ by ___ thy ___ light glow - ing,

Show to us beau - ty, ___ vi - sion ___ and joy.

Scotland's Burning

Scot - land's burn - ing, Scot - land's burn - ing, Look yon - der! Look yon - der!

Fire, fire, fire, fire! Pour on wa - ter, pour on wa - ter.

Shalom Chaverim

Israeli Round

Sha - lom, cha - ve - rim! Sha - lom, cha - ve - rim! Sha - lom, sha - lom! Le -
Fare - well, good _ friends! Fare - well, good _ friends! Fare - well, fare - well! Till we

hit - ra - ot, le - hit - ra - ot, sha - lom, sha - lom.
meet a - gain, till we meet a - gain, fare - well, fare - well.

270

Summer Is A-Coming In
(Sumer Is A-Comin In)

Old English*

(2-6 parts)

Sum - mer is a - com - ing in,___ Loud - ly sing cuck - oo,___
Su - mer is a - cu - men in,___ Lhu - de sing cuc - cu!

Grow - eth seed and blow - eth mead, And spring - eth wood a - new.___ Sing, cuck -
Grow - eth sed and blow - eth med, And spring - eth wo - de nu.___ Sing, cuc -

oo. Ewe now bleat - eth af - ter lamb. For calf now low - eth cow.
cu! Aw - e ble - teth af - ter lomb. Lhouth af - ter cal - ve cu;

Bull - ock rous - eth, buck he brow - seth, Mer - ry sing cuck - oo. Cuck - oo,
Bul - loc ster - teth, buck - e ver - teth, Mur - ie sing cuc - cu. Cuc - cu,

cuck - oo,___ Well thou sing - est cuck - oo, O ne'er be si - lent now.
cuc - cu!___ Wel sing - es thu cuc - cu, Ne swik thu nav - er nu!

*This is one of the earliest rounds (rotas).

For Further Study

Listed below are several publications that may be used to further the vocal development of beginning and intermediate voice students. They are also useful in acquainting students with different styles of song. Much of this music is available in two or more volumes and high and low keys.

Title	Editor or Composer	Publisher
All Sondheim	Sondheim	Revelation
American Folksongs Collection		G. Schirmer
Anthology of French Song	Spicker	G. Schirmer
Complete Vocal Selections from 10 Broadway Shows		Columbia Picture Productions
Ballad Book, The	Niles	Dover
Best of Broadway		Hansen House
Broadway Platinum (Ultimate)		Hal Leonard
Broadway Repertoire		Chappell
18th Century Italian Songs	Fuchs	International
Folksong Arrangements	Britten	Boosey & Hawkes
45 Arias	Handel	International
42 Folk Songs	Brahms	International
Heritage Songster	Dallin	Wm. C. Brown
Heritage of 20th Century British Song, A		Boosey & Hawkes
Irish Country Songs	Hughes	Boosey & Hawkes
Old American Songs	Copland	Boosey & Hawkes
Reliquary of English Song	Potter	G. Schirmer
36 Arie di Stile Antico	Donaudy	Ricordi
Singers' Musical Theatre Anthology		Hal Leonard

Glossary of Musical Terms and Symbols

The terms listed are used in the songs contained in the anthology of this text.

accel. **Accelerando.** Accelerate tempo.

Adagio sostenuto. Slow, sustained tempo.

Allegretto. Tempo between allegro and andante.

Allegro. Lively, rapid.

Allegro maestoso. Rapid but majestic.

Allegro ma non troppo. Lively, but not too rapid.

Andante. Moderate, "walking" speed.

Andante con moto. Slow, with flowing movement.

Andante sostenuto. Slow and sustained.

Andante tranquillo. Slow and peaceful.

Andantino molto cantabile. Rather slow and very songlike.

A tempo. Resume original tempo.

Coda. A "tail," a short passage ending a musical composition.

Colla voce. Follow the voice.

Con tenerezza. With tenderness.

<	**Crescendo.** Gradually increase volume.
D.C.	**Da capo.** Go back to the beginning of the song.
S	**Dal segno.** Go back to the sign.
>	**Descrescendo.** Gradually decrease volume.
dim.	**Diminuendo.** Gradually decrease volume.
	Expressivo. Expressively.
⌒	**Fermata.** Hold.
	Fine. Sing to the end or to the word **Fine.**
f	**Forte.** Loud.
ff	**Fortissimo.** Very loud.
	Interlude. Music played between sections of a song or aria.
	Langsam. Slow.
	Larghetto. Quite slow.
	Largo. The slowest tempo marking.
	Legato. Connected, smooth.
	Lento. Slow.
	Lunga. Sustained.
	Meno mosso. Not so fast.
	Mezza voce. With half the power of the voice.
	Mezzo forte. Medium loud.
	Mezzo piano. Medium quiet.
	Moderato. Moderately fast.
	Molto legato. Very smooth.
	Morendo. Dying.
pp	**Pianissimo.** Very quiet.
p	**Piano.** Quiet.
	Piu espressivo. More expressively.
	Piu mosso. More movement, faster.
	Poco. A little.
poco rit.	**Poco ritardando.** Slightly decreasing tempo.

rall.	***Rallentando.*** Gradually decreasing tempo.
	Refrain. A repeated section of music.
rit.	***Ritardando.*** Gradually decreasing tempo.
rit. essen. assai	Ritardando essenziale assai. A significant ritard.
	Sempre crescendo. Continually increasing volume.
sf	***Sforzando.*** Sudden emphasis.
	Ziemlich langsam. Rather slow.

Glossary of
Technical Terms

ANATOMY	Study of the structure of the human body.
ANGLE	Projection formed by two diverging surfaces.
ARTICULATION	Process of pronouncing a sound.
ARYTENOID	One of a pair of triangular-shaped cartilages attached to the cricoid cartilage. Posteriorally, the vocal cords are joined to them.
"BREAK"	An interruption in the normal production of sound, caused by muscle spasm.
BRONCHIOLE	Smallest subdivision of the trachea, through which oxygen passes into the lungs.
BRONCHUS (bronchi, pl.)	Subdivision of the trachea, one branch penetrating each lung.
CARTILAGE	Tissue having the capability of developing into bone.
"CHEST" REGISTER	Lowest register in the male and female range.
COCHLEA	Spiral bony tube, located in the inner ear, containing nerve endings necessary for hearing.
COMPRESSION	Outward pushing of the air molecules in the production of sound.
CRICOID	Lower circular cartilage of the larynx.

DIAPHRAGM	Massive, dome-shaped muscle dividing the chest cavity from the abdominal cavity.
DICTION	Clarity and distinctness of speech or singing.
DURATION	Length of time a sound is heard.
EAR CANAL	Tube leading from the outer ear to the eardrum
EARDRUM	Membrane that oscillates at the same frequency with which it is disturbed by air waves.
EPIGLOTTIS	Leaf-shaped cartilage that serves as a "lid" to the larynx.
FALSETTO	Highest register in the male voice.
FOCUS	Term borrowed from optics, referring to the clarity of tone.
FUNDAMENTAL	The perceived pitch of a musical sound. Musical spectra consist of many different frequencies, called overtones.
GLOTTAL FRY	Creaky-sounding extreme low part of the voice.
HARD PALATE	Anterior bony portion of the roof of the mouth.
HARMONIC	A special class of overtones that are whole-number multiples of the fundamental pitch.
"HEAD" REGISTER	Highest of the main registers in the female voice, middle register of the male voice.
INNER EAR	Cavity containing structures essential for hearing, primarily the cochlea.
INTENSITY	"Core" or concentration of sound within a tone, which gives it "carrying power," brilliance.
INTERCOSTAL MUSCLES	Groups of muscles that raise and lower ribs.
INVOLUNTARY	Term applied to a muscle that cannot be willfully controlled.
LARYNX	Voice box.

LUNGS	Pair of membranous sacs located in the chest.
MASSETER	"Chewing" muscles.
MEMBRANE	Thin, supple tissue that serves as a covering to structures in the body.
MIDDLE EAR	Portion of the ear containing the ear canal and eardrum.
MIDDLE REGISTER	Middle register in the female voice.
MUSCLE	Bundles of fibers that can contract and relax, resulting in bodily movement.
NOISE	Acoustical term referring to sound that emits uneven sound wave.
OSSICLES	Three small bones suspended between the eardrum and oval window.
OVAL WINDOW	Membrane in the wall of the cochlea that, when vibrating, sets into motion the fluid in the cochlea.
PARTIAL	In most cases, an alternative term for harmonic.
PHYSIOLOGY	Study of the functions of the parts of the human body.
PITCH	The perceived musical note, determined in part by the number of times a sound wave oscillates the ear drum.
RAREFACTION	The bouncing back toward the sound source of the elastic air molecules after they have been compressed.
REGISTER	A series of succeeding vocal sounds of equal quality on a scale that differs from another series of succeeding sounds of equal quality.
RESONANCE	Intensification and prolongation of sound.
RESONATOR	Sympathetically vibrating surface or cavity that amplifies and dampens partials.
SOFT PALATE	Muscular membranous section in the roof of the mouth behind hard palate.

SONANT	Consonant that contains vowel sound.
STERNUM	Breastbone.
SURD	Voiceless consonant.
THORAX	Chest.
THYROARYTE-NOID	A pair of muscles that course from the thyroid to the arytenoids. The vocal cords are part of this group.
THYROID	Upper V-shaped cartilage of the larynx.
TIMBRE	See tone.
TONE	Timbre, or the identifying quality of a sound. Tone is largely dependent on the overtone content of the sound.
TRACHEA	Windpipe.
VOCAL CORDS	A pair of musclar folds that vibrate when air passes through them, thereby producing sound.
WHISTLE REGISTER	Highest register in the female voice.

International Phonetic Alphabet

spellings	IPA	spellings	IPA
pat	æ	sauce	s
pay	e	ship, dish	ʃ
care	ɛr, er	tight, stopped	t
father	ɑ:, ɑ	thin	θ
bib	b	this	ð
church	tʃ	cut	ʌ
deed, milled	d	urge, term, firm,	ɜ; ɜr
pet	ɛ	word, heard	
bee	i	valve	v
fife, phase	f	with	w
gag	g	yes	j
hat	h	zebra, xylem	z
which	hw (also ʍ)	vision, pleasure,	ʒ
pit	ɪ	garage	
pie, by	aɪ	about, item, edible,	ə
pier	ɪr, ir	gallop, circus	
judge	dʒ	butter	ɚ
kick, cat, pique	k		
lid, needle	l, l̩ [ˈnidl̩]	FOREIGN	
mum	m		IPA
no, sudden	n, n̩ [ˈsʌdn̩]		
thing	ŋ	*French* ami	a
pot, *horrid	ɑ	*French* feu,	œ
toe, *hoarse	o	*German* schön	
caught, paw, *for	ɔ	*French* tu,	y
noise	ɔɪ	*German* über	
took	ʊ	*German* ich,	x
boot	u	*Scottish* loch	
out	aʊ	*French* bon	õ, æ̃, ɑ̃, œ̃
pop	p	*French* compiègne	ɲ
roar	r		

Index